THE PELICAN SHAKESPEARE
GENERAL EDITORS

STEPHEN ORGEL
A. R. BRAUNMULLER

The Merry Wives of Windsor

The American comedian James Henry Hackett as Falstaff.
A Shakespeare scholar as well as an actor, Hackett was the
first American to become a major star on the English stage. His
Merry Wives was produced in London in 1851, to great acclaim.
(Courtesy of the Stanford University Library)

William Shakespeare

The Merry Wives
of Windsor

EDITED BY RUSS McDONALD

PENGUIN BOOKS

PENGUIN BOOKS

Published by the Penguin Group

Penguin Group (USA) Inc., 375 Hudson Street, New York, New York 10014, U.S.A.

Penguin Books Ltd, 80 Strand, London WC2R 0RL, England

Penguin Books Australia Ltd, 250 Camberwell Road, Camberwell, Victoria 3124, Australia

Penguin Books Canada Ltd, 10 Alcorn Avenue, Toronto, Ontario, Canada M4V 3B2

Penguin Books India (P) Ltd, 11 Community Centre, Panchsheel Park, New Delhi – 110 017, India

Penguin Group (NZ), cnr Airborne and Rosedale Roads, Albany, Auckland 1310, New Zealand

Penguin Books (South Africa) (Pty) Ltd, 24 Sturdee Avenue,
Rosebank, Johannesburg 2196, South Africa

Penguin Books Ltd, Registered Offices: 80 Strand, London WC2R 0RL, England

The Merry Wives of Windsor edited by Fredson Bowers
published in the United States of America in Penguin Books 1963
Revised edition published 1979
This new edition edited by Russ McDonald published 2002

14 16 18 20 19 17 15 13

Copyright © Penguin Books Inc., 1963
Copyright © Viking Penguin Inc., 1979
Copyright © Penguin Putnam Inc., 2002
All rights reserved

LIBRARY OF CONGRESS CATALOGING IN PUBLICATION DATA
Shakespeare, William, 1564–1616.
The merry wives of Windsor / William Shakespeare ; edited with an
introduction by Russ McDonald.
p. cm.—(The Pelican Shakespeare)
ISBN 0 14 07.1464 2 (pbk. : alk. paper)
1. Falstaff, John, Sir (Fictitious character)—Drama. 2. Windsor
(Berkshire, England)—Drama. 3. Married women—Drama.
I. McDonald, Russ, 1949– II. Title. III. Series.
PR2826.A2 M33 2002
822.3'3—dc21 2001054854

Printed in the United States of America
Set in Adobe Garamond
Designed by Virginia Norey

Except in the United States of America, this book is sold subject
to the condition that it shall not, by way of trade or otherwise, be lent,
re-sold, hired out, or otherwise circulated without the publisher's prior
consent in any form of binding or cover other than that in which
it is published and without a similar condition including this
condition being imposed on the subsequent purchaser.

Contents

Publisher's Note

IT IS ALMOST half a century since the first volumes of the Pelican Shakespeare appeared under the general editorship of Alfred Harbage. The fact that a new edition, rather than simply a revision, has been undertaken reflects the profound changes textual and critical studies of Shakespeare have undergone in the past twenty years. For the new Pelican series, the texts of the plays and poems have been thoroughly revised in accordance with recent scholarship, and in some cases have been entirely reedited. New introductions and notes have been provided in all the volumes. But the new Shakespeare is also designed as a successor to the original series; the previous editions have been taken into account, and the advice of the previous editors has been solicited where it was feasible to do so.

Certain textual features of the new Pelican Shakespeare should be particularly noted. All lines are numbered that contain a word, phrase, or allusion explained in the glossarial notes. In addition, for convenience, every tenth line is also numbered, in italics when no annotation is indicated. The intrusive and often inaccurate place headings inserted by early editors are omitted (as is becoming standard practice), but for the convenience of those who miss them, an indication of locale now appears as the first item in the annotation of each scene.

In the interest of both elegance and utility, each speech prefix is set in a separate line when the speaker's lines are in verse, except when those words form the second half of a verse line. Thus the verse form of the speech is kept visually intact. What is printed as verse and what is printed as prose has, in general, the authority of the original texts. Departures from the original texts in this regard have only the authority of editorial tradition and the judgment of the Pelican editors; and, in a few instances, are admittedly arbitrary.

The Theatrical World

Economic REALITIES determined the theatrical world in which Shakespeare's plays were written, performed, and received. For centuries in England, the primary theatrical tradition was nonprofessional. Craft guilds (or "mysteries") provided religious drama – mystery plays – as part of the celebration of religious and civic festivals, and schools and universities staged classical and neoclassical drama in both Latin and English as part of their curricula. In these forms, drama was established and socially acceptable. Professional theater, in contrast, existed on the margins of society. The acting companies were itinerant; playhouses could be any available space – the great halls of the aristocracy, town squares, civic halls, inn yards, fair booths, or open fields – and income was sporadic, dependent on the passing of the hat or on the bounty of local patrons. The actors, moreover, were considered little better than vagabonds, constantly in danger of arrest or expulsion.

In the late 1560s and 1570s, however, English professional theater began to gain respectability. Wealthy aristocrats fond of drama – the Lord Admiral, for example, or the Lord Chamberlain – took acting companies under their protection so that the players technically became members of their households and were no longer subject to arrest as homeless or masterless men. Permanent theaters were first built at this time as well, allowing the companies to control and charge for entry to their performances.

Shakespeare's livelihood, and the stunning artistic explosion in which he participated, depended on pragmatic and architectural effort. Professional theater requires ways to restrict access to its offerings; if it does not, and admission fees cannot be charged, the actors do not get paid, the costumes go to a pawnbroker, and there is no such thing as a professional, ongoing theatrical tradition. The answer to that economic need arrived in the late 1560s and 1570s with the creation of the so-called public or amphitheater playhouse. Recent discoveries indicate that the precursor of the Globe playhouse in London (where Shakespeare's mature plays were presented) and the Rose theater (which presented Christopher Marlowe's plays and some of Shakespeare's earliest ones) was the Red Lion theater of 1567. Archaeological studies of the foundations of the Rose and Globe theaters have revealed that the open-air theater of the 1590s and later was probably a polygonal building with fourteen to twenty or twenty-four sides, multistoried, from 75 to 100 feet in diameter, with a raised, partly covered "thrust" stage that projected into a group of standing patrons, or "groundlings," and a covered gallery, seating up to 2,500 or more (very crowded) spectators.

These theaters might have been about half full on any given day, though the audiences were larger on holidays or when a play was advertised, as old and new were, through printed playbills posted around London. The metropolitan area's late-Tudor, early-Stuart population (circa 1590-1620) has been estimated at about 150,000 to 250,000. It has been supposed that in the mid-1590s there were about 15,000 spectators per week at the public theaters; thus, as many as 10 percent of the local population went to the theater regularly. Consequently, the theaters' repertories – the plays available for this experienced and frequent audience – had to change often: in the month between September 15 and October 15, 1595, for instance, the Lord Admiral's Men performed twenty-eight times in eighteen different plays.

Since natural light illuminated the amphitheaters' stages, performances began between noon and two o'clock and ran without a break for two or three hours. They often concluded with a jig, a fencing display, or some other nondramatic exhibition. Weather conditions deter-

mined the season for the amphitheaters: plays were performed every day (including Sundays, sometimes, to cler-
ical dismay) except during Lent – the forty days before
Easter – or periods of plague, or sometimes during the
summer months when law courts were not in session and
the most affluent members of the audience were not in
London.

To a modern theatergoer, an amphitheater stage like
that of the Rose or Globe would appear an unfamiliar mixture of plainness and elaborate decoration. Much of the
structure was carved or painted, sometimes to imitate
marble; elsewhere, as under the canopy projecting over the
stage, to represent the stars and the zodiac. Appropriate
painted canvas pictures (of Jerusalem, for example, if the
play was set in that city) were apparently hung on the wall
behind the acting area, and tragedies were accompanied by
black hangings, presumably something like crepe festoons
or bunting. Although these theaters did not employ what
we would call scenery, early modern spectators saw numerous large props, such as the "bar" at which a prisoner stood
during a trial, the "mossy bank" where lovers reclined,
an arbor for amorous conversation, a chariot, gallows,
tables, trees, beds, thrones, writing desks, and so forth.
Audiences might learn a scene's location from a sign (reading "Athens," for example) carried across the stage (as in
Bertolt Brecht's twentieth-century productions). Equally
captivating (and equally irritating to the theater's enemies)
were the rich costumes and personal props the actors used:
the most valuable items in the surviving theatrical invento-
ries are the swords, gowns, robes, crowns, and other items
worn or carried by the performers.

Magic appealed to Shakespeare's audiences as much as
it does to us today, and the theater exploited many decep-
tive and spectacular devices. A winch in the loft above the
stage, called "the heavens," could lower and raise actors
playing gods, goddesses, and other supernatural figures to
and from the main acting area, just as one or more trap-
doors permitted entrances and exits to and from the area,

called "hell," beneath the stage. Actors wore elementary makeup such as wigs, false beards, and face paint, and they employed pig's bladders filled with animal blood to make wounds seem more real. They had rudimentary but effective ways of pretending to behead or hang a person. Supernumeraries (stagehands or actors not needed in a particular scene) could make thunder sounds (by shaking a metal sheet or rolling an iron ball down a chute) and show lightning (by blowing inflammable resin through tubes into a flame). Elaborate fireworks enhanced the effects of dragons flying through the air or imitated such celestial phenomena as comets, shooting stars, and multiple suns. Horses' hoofbeats, bells (located perhaps in the tower above the stage), trumpets and drums, clocks, cannon shots and gunshots, and the like were common sound effects. And the music of viols, cornets, oboes, and recorders was a regular feature of theatrical performances.

For two relatively brief spans, from the late 1570s to 1590 and from 1599 to 1614, the amphitheaters competed with the so-called private, or indoor, theaters, which originated as, or later represented themselves as, educational institutions training boys as singers for church services and court performances. These indoor theaters had two features that were distinct from the amphitheaters': their personnel and their playing spaces. The amphitheaters' adult companies included both adult men, who played the male roles, and boys, who played the female roles; the private, or indoor, theater companies, on the other hand, were entirely composed of boys aged about 8 to 16, who were, or could pretend to be, candidates for singers in a church or a royal boys' choir. (Until 1660, professional theatrical companies included no women.) The playing space would appear much more familiar to modern audiences than the long-vanished amphitheaters; the later indoor theaters were, in fact, the ancestors of the typical modern theater. They were enclosed spaces, usually rectangular, with the stage filling one end of the rectangle and the audience arrayed in seats or benches across (and sometimes lining) the building's longer axis. These spaces staged plays less frequently than the public theaters (perhaps only once a week) and held far fewer spectators than the amphitheaters: about 200 to 600, as opposed to 2,500 or more. Fewer patrons mean a smaller gross income, unless each pays more. Not surprisingly, then, private theaters charged higher prices than the amphitheaters, probably sixpence, as opposed to a penny for the cheapest entry.

Protected from the weather, the indoor theaters presented plays later in the day than the amphitheaters, and used artificial illumination – candles in sconces or candelabra. But candles melt, and need replacing, snuffing, and trimming, and these practical requirements may have been part of the reason the indoor theaters introduced breaks in the performance, the intermission so dear to the heart of theatergoers and to the pocketbooks of theater concessionaires ever since. Whether motivated by the need to tend to the candles or by the entrepreneurs' wishing to sell oranges and liquor, or both, the indoor theaters eventually established the modern convention of the non-continuous performance. In the early modern "private" theater, musical performances apparently filled the intermissions, which in Stuart theater jargon seem to have been called "acts."

At the end of the first decade of the seventeenth century, the distinction between public amphitheaters and private indoor companies ceased. For various cultural, political, and economic reasons, individual companies gained control of both the public, open-air theaters and the indoor ones, and companies mixing adult men and boys took over the formerly "private" theaters. Despite the death of the boys' companies and of their highly innovative theaters (for which such luminous playwrights as Ben Jonson, George Chapman, and John Marston wrote), their playing spaces and conventions had an immense impact on subsequent plays: not merely for the intervals (which stressed the artistic and architectonic importance of "acts"), but also because they introduced political and social satire as a popular dramatic ingredient, even in tragedy, and a wider range of actorly effects, encouraged by their more intimate playing spaces.

Even the briefest sketch of the Shakespearean theatrical world would be incomplete without some comment on the social and cultural dimensions of theaters and playing in the period. In an intensely hierarchical and status-conscious society, professional actors and their ventures had hardly any respectability; as we have indicated, to protect themselves against laws designed to curb vagabondage and the increase of masterless men, actors resorted to the near-fiction that they were the servants of noble masters, and wore their distinctive livery. Hence the company for which Shakespeare wrote in the 1590s called itself the Lord Chamberlain's Men and pretended that the public, money-getting performances were in fact rehearsals for private performances before that high court official. From 1598, the Privy Council had licensed theatrical companies, and after 1603, with the accession of King James I, the companies gained explicit royal protection, just as the Queen's Men had for a time under Queen Elizabeth. The Chamberlain's Men became the King's Men, and the other companies were patronized by the other members of the royal family.

These designations were legal fictions that half-concealed an important economic and social development, the evolution away from the theater's organization on the model of the guild, a self-regulating confraternity of individual artisans, into a proto-capitalist organization. Shakespeare's company became a joint-stock company, where persons who supplied capital and, in some cases, such as Shakespeare's, capital and talent, employed themselves and others in earning a return on that capital. This development meant that actors and theater companies were outside both the traditional guild structures, which required some form of civic or royal charter, and the feudal household organization of master-and-servant. This anomalous, maverick social and economic condition made theater companies practically unruly and potentially even dangerous; consequently, numerous official bodies – including the London metropolitan and ecclesiastical authorities as well as, occasionally, the royal court itself – tried, without much success, to control and even to disband them.

Public officials had good reason to want to close the theaters: they were attractive nuisances – they drew often riotous crowds, they were always noisy, and they could be politically offensive and socially insubordinate. Until the Civil War, however, anti-theatrical forces failed to shut down professional theater, for many reasons – limited surveillance and few police powers, tensions or outright hostilities among the agencies that sought to check or channel theatrical activity, and lack of clear policies for control. Another reason must have been the theaters' undeniable popularity. Curtailing any activity enjoyed by such a substantial percentage of the population was difficult, as various Roman emperors attempting to limit circuses had learned, and the Tudor-Stuart audience was not merely large, it was socially diverse and included women. The prevalence of public entertainment in this period has been underestimated. In fact, fairs, holidays, games, sporting events, the equivalent of modern parades, freak shows, and street exhibitions all abounded, but the theater was the most widely and frequently available entertainment to which people of every class had access. That fact helps account both for its quantity and for the fear and anger it aroused.

WILLIAM SHAKESPEARE OF
STRATFORD-UPON-AVON, GENTLEMAN

Many people have said that we know very little about William Shakespeare's life – pinheads and postcards are often mentioned as appropriately tiny surfaces on which to record the available information. More imaginatively and perhaps more correctly, Ralph Waldo Emerson wrote, "Shakespeare is the only biographer of Shakespeare. . . . So far from Shakespeare's being the least known, he is the one person in all modern history fully known to us."

In fact, we know more about Shakespeare's life than we do about almost any other English writer's of his era. His last will and testament (dated March 25, 1616) survives, as do numerous legal contracts and court documents involving Shakespeare as principal or witness, and parish records in Stratford and London. Shakespeare appears quite often in official records of King James's royal court, and of course Shakespeare's name appears on numerous title pages and in the written and recorded words of his literary contemporaries Robert Greene, Henry Chettle, Francis Meres, John Davies of Hereford, Ben Jonson, and many others. Indeed, if we make due allowance for the bloating of modern, run-of-the-mill bureaucratic records, more information has survived over the past four hundred years about William Shakespeare of Stratford-upon-Avon, Warwickshire, than is likely to survive in the next four hundred years about any reader of these words.

What we do not have are entire categories of information – Shakespeare's private letters or diaries, drafts and revisions of poems and plays, critical prefaces or essays, commendatory verse for other writers' works, or instructions guiding his fellow actors in their performances, for instance – that we imagine would help us understand and appreciate his surviving writings. For all we know, many such data never existed as written records. Many literary and theatrical critics, not knowing what might once have existed, more or less cheerfully accept the situation; some even make a theoretical virtue of it by claiming that such data are irrelevant to understanding and interpreting the plays and poems.

So, what do we know about William Shakespeare, the man responsible for thirty-seven or perhaps more plays, more than 150 sonnets, two lengthy narrative poems, and some shorter poems?

While many families by the name of Shakespeare (or some variant spelling) can be identified in the English Midlands as far back as the twelfth century, it seems likely that the dramatist's grandfather, Richard, moved to Snitterfield, a town not far from Stratford-upon-Avon, sometime before 1529. In Snitterfield, Richard Shakespeare leased farmland from the very wealthy Robert Arden. By 1552, Richard's son John had moved to a large house on Henley Street in Stratford-upon-Avon, the house that stands today as "The Birthplace." In Stratford, John Shakespeare traded as a glover, dealt in wool, and lent money at interest; he also served in a variety of civic posts, including "High Bailiff," the municipality's equivalent of mayor. In 1557, he married Robert Arden's youngest daughter, Mary. Mary and John had four sons – William was the oldest – and four daughters, of whom only Joan outlived her most celebrated sibling. William was baptized (an event entered in the Stratford parish church records) on April 26, 1564, and it has become customary, without any good factual support, to suppose he was born on April 23, which happens to be the feast day of Saint George, patron saint of England, and is also the date on which he died, in 1616. Shakespeare married Anne Hathaway in 1582, when he was eighteen and she was twenty-six; their first child was born five months later. It has been generally assumed that the marriage was enforced and subsequently unhappy, but these are only assumptions; it has been estimated, for instance, that up to one third of Elizabethan brides were pregnant when they married. Anne and William Shakespeare had three children: Susanna, who married a prominent local physician, John Hall; and the twins Hamnet, who died young in 1596, and Judith, who married Thomas Quiney – apparently a rather shady individual. The name Hamnet was unusual but not unique: he and his twin sister were named for their godparents, Shakespeare's neighbors Hamnet and Judith Sadler. Shakespeare's father died in 1601 (the year of *Hamlet*), and Mary Arden Shakespeare died in 1608 (the year of *Coriolanus*). William Shakespeare's last surviving direct descendant was his granddaughter Elizabeth Hall, who died in 1670.

Between the birth of the twins in 1585 and a clear reference to Shakespeare as a practicing London dramatist in Robert Greene's sensationalizing, satiric pamphlet, *Greene's Groatsworth of Wit* (1592), there is no record of where William Shakespeare was or what he was doing. These seven so-called lost years have been imaginatively filled by scholars and other students of Shakespeare: some think he traveled to Italy, or fought in the Low Countries, or studied law or medicine, or worked as an apprentice actor/writer, and so on to even more fanciful possibilities. Whatever the biographical facts for those "lost" years, Greene's nasty remarks in 1592 testify to professional envy and to the fact that Shakespeare already had a successful career in London. Speaking to his fellow playwrights, Greene warns both generally and specifically:

> . . . trust them [actors] not: for there is an upstart crow, beautified with our feathers, that with his tiger's heart wrapped in a player's hide supposes he is as well able to bombast out a blank verse as the best of you; and being an absolute Johannes Factotum, is in his own conceit the only Shake-scene in a country.

The passage mimics a line from *3 Henry VI* (hence the play must have been performed before Greene wrote) and seems to say that "Shake-scene" is both actor and playwright, a jack-of-all-trades. That same year, Henry Chettle protested Greene's remarks in *Kind-Heart's Dream,* and each of the next two years saw the publication of poems — *Venus and Adonis* and *The Rape of Lucrece,* respectively — publicly ascribed to (and dedicated by) Shakespeare. Early in 1595 he was named as one of the senior members of a prominent acting company, the Lord Chamberlain's Men, when they received payment for court performances during the 1594 Christmas season.

Clearly, Shakespeare had achieved both success and reputation in London. In 1596, upon Shakespeare's application, the College of Arms granted his father the now-familiar coat of arms he had taken the first steps to obtain almost twenty years before, and in 1598, John's son – now permitted to call himself "gentleman" – took a 10 percent share in the new Globe playhouse. In 1597, he bought a substantial bourgeois house, called New Place, in Stratford – the garden remains, but Shakespeare's house, several times rebuilt, was torn down in 1759 – and over the next few years Shakespeare spent large sums buying land and making other investments in the town and its environs. Though he worked in London, his family remained in Stratford, and he seems always to have considered Stratford the home he would eventually return to. Something approaching a disinterested appreciation of Shakespeare's popular and professional status appears in Francis Meres's *Palladis Tamia* (1598), a not especially imaginative and perhaps therefore persuasive record of literary reputations. Reviewing contemporary English writers, Meres lists the titles of many of Shakespeare's plays, including one not now known, *Love's Labor's Won*, and praises his "mellifluous & hony-tongued" "sugred Sonnets," which were then circulating in manuscript (they were first collected in 1609). Meres describes Shakespeare as "one of the best" English playwrights of both comedy and tragedy. In *Remains . . . Concerning Britain* (1605), William Camden – a more authoritative source than the imitative Meres – calls Shakespeare one of the "most pregnant witts of these our times" and joins him with such writers as Chapman, Daniel, Jonson, Marston, and Spenser. During the first decades of the seventeenth century, publishers began to attribute numerous play quartos, including some non-Shakespearean ones, to Shakespeare, either by name or initials, and we may assume that they deemed Shakespeare's name and supposed authorship, true or false, commercially attractive.

For the next ten years or so, various records show

Shakespeare's dual career as playwright and man of the theater in London, and as an important local figure in Stratford. In 1608-9 his acting company – designated the "King's Men" soon after King James had succeeded Queen Elizabeth in 1603 – rented, refurbished, and opened a small interior playing space, the Blackfriars theater, in London, and Shakespeare was once again listed as a substantial sharer in the group of proprietors of the playhouse. By May 11, 1612, however, he describes himself as a Stratford resident in a London lawsuit – an indication that he had withdrawn from day-to-day professional activity and returned to the town where he had always had his main financial interests. When Shakespeare bought a substantial residential building in London, the Blackfriars Gatehouse, close to the theater of the same name, on March 10, 1613, he is recorded as William Shakespeare "of Stratford upon Avon in the county of Warwick, gentleman," and he named several London residents as the building's trustees. Still, he continued to participate in theatrical activity: when the new Earl of Rutland needed an allegorical design to bear as a shield, or *impresa*, at the celebration of King James's Accession Day, March 24, 1613, the earl's accountant recorded a payment of 44 shillings to Shakespeare for the device with its motto.

For the last few years of his life, Shakespeare evidently concentrated his activities in the town of his birth. Most of the final records concern business transactions in Stratford, ending with the notation of his death on April 23, 1616, and burial in Holy Trinity Church, Stratford-upon-Avon.

THE QUESTION OF AUTHORSHIP

The history of ascribing Shakespeare's plays (the poems do not come up so often) to someone else began, as it continues, peculiarly. The earliest published claim that someone else wrote Shakespeare's plays appeared in an 1856 article by Delia Bacon in the American journal *Putnam's Monthly* – although an Englishman, Thomas Wilmot, had shared his doubts in private (even secretive) conversations with friends near the end of the eighteenth century. Bacon's was a sad personal history that ended in madness and poverty, but the year after her article, she published, with great difficulty and the bemused assistance of Nathaniel Hawthorne (then United States Consul in Liverpool, England), her *Philosophy of the Plays of Shakspere Unfolded*. This huge, ornately written, confusing farrago is almost unreadable; sometimes its intents, to say nothing of its arguments, disappear entirely beneath near-raving, ecstatic writing. Tumbled in with much supposed "philosophy" appear the claims that Francis Bacon (from whom Delia Bacon eventually claimed descent), Walter Ralegh, and several other contemporaries of Shakespeare's had written the plays. The book had little impact except as a ridiculed curiosity.

Once proposed, however, the issue gained momentum among people whose conviction was the greater in proportion to their ignorance of sixteenth- and seventeenth-century English literature, history, and society. Another American amateur, Catherine P. Ashmead Windle, made the next influential contribution to the cause when she published *Report to the British Museum* (1882), wherein she promised to open "the Cipher of Francis Bacon," though what she mostly offers, in the words of S. Schoenbaum, is "demented allegorizing." An entire new cottage industry grew from Windle's suggestion that the texts contain hidden, cryptographically discoverable ciphers – "clues" – to their authorship; and today there are not only books devoted to the putative ciphers, but also pamphlets, journals, and newsletters.

Although Baconians have led the pack of those seeking a substitute Shakespeare, in *"Shakespeare" Identified* (1920), J. Thomas Looney became the first published

"Oxfordian" when he proposed Edward de Vere, seven-teenth earl of Oxford, as the secret author of Shakespeare's plays. Also for Oxford and his "authorship" there are today dedicated societies, articles, journals, and books. Less popular candidates – Queen Elizabeth and Christo-pher Marlowe among them – have had adherents, but the movement seems to have divided into two main contend-ing factions, Baconian and Oxfordian. (For further details on all the candidates for "Shakespeare," see S. Schoen-baum, *Shakespeare's Lives,* 2nd ed., 1991.)

The Baconians, the Oxfordians, and supporters of other candidates have one trait in common – they are snobs. Every pro-Bacon or pro-Oxford tract sooner or later claims that the historical William Shakespeare of Stratford-upon-Avon could not have written the plays be-cause he could not have had the training, the university education, the experience, and indeed the imagination or background their author supposedly possessed. Only a learned genius like Bacon or an aristocrat like Oxford could have written such fine plays. (As it happens, lucky male children of the middle class had access to better edu-cation than most aristocrats in Elizabethan England – and Oxford was not particularly well educated.) Shake-speare received in the Stratford grammar school a formal education that would daunt many college graduates today; and popular rival playwrights such as the very learned Ben Jonson and George Chapman, both of whom also lacked university training, achieved great artistic suc-cess, without being taken as Bacon or Oxford.

Besides snobbery, one other quality characterizes the authorship controversy: lack of evidence. A great deal of testimony from Shakespeare's time shows that Shake-speare wrote Shakespeare's plays and that his contempo-raries recognized them as distinctive and distinctly superior. (Some of that contemporary evidence is col-lected in E. K. Chambers, *William Shakespeare: A Study of Facts and Problems,* 2 vols., 1930.) Since that testimony comes from Shakespeare's enemies and theatrical competitors as well as from his co-workers and from the Elizabethan equivalent of literary journalists, it seems unlikely that, if any of these sources had known he was a fraud, they would have failed to record that fact.

Books About Shakespeare's Theater

Useful scholarly studies of theatrical life in Shakespeare's day include: G. E. Bentley, *The Jacobean and Caroline Stage,* 7 vols. (1941-68), and the same author's *The Professions of Dramatist and Player in Shakespeare's Time, 1590-1642* (1986); E. K. Chambers, *The Elizabethan Stage,* 4 vols. (1923); R. A. Foakes, *Illustrations of the English Stage, 1580-1642* (1985); Andrew Gurr, *The Shakespearean Stage,* 3rd ed. (1992), and the same author's *Play-going in Shakespeare's London,* 2nd ed. (1996); Edwin Nungezer, *A Dictionary of Actors* (1929); Carol Chillington Rutter, ed., *Documents of the Rose Playhouse* (1984).

Books About Shakespeare's Life

The following books provide scholarly, documented accounts of Shakespeare's life: G. E. Bentley, *Shakespeare: A Biographical Handbook* (1961); E. K. Chambers, *William Shakespeare: A Study of Facts and Problems,* 2 vols. (1930); S. Schoenbaum, *William Shakespeare: A Compact Documentary Life* (1977); and *Shakespeare's Lives,* 2nd ed. (1991), by the same author. Many scholarly editions of Shakespeare's complete works print brief compilations of essential dates and events. References to Shakespeare's works up to 1700 are collected in C. M. Ingleby et al., *The Shakespeare Allusion-Book,* rev. ed., 2 vols. (1932).

The Texts of Shakespeare

As FAR AS WE KNOW, only one manuscript conceivably in Shakespeare's own hand may (and even this is much disputed) exist: a few pages of a play called *Sir Thomas More*, which apparently was never performed. What we do have, as later readers, performers, scholars, students, are printed texts. The earliest of these survive in two forms: quartos and folios. Quartos (from the Latin for "four") are small books, printed on sheets of paper that were then folded in fours, to make eight double-sided pages. When these were bound together, the result was a squarish, eminently portable volume that sold for the relatively small sum of sixpence (translating in modern terms to about $5.00). In folios, on the other hand, the sheets are folded only once, in half, producing large, impressive volumes taller than they are wide. This was the format for important works of philosophy, science, theology, and literature (the major precedent for a folio Shakespeare was Ben Jonson's *Works,* 1616). The decision to print the works of a popular playwright in folio is an indication of how far up on the social scale the theatrical profession had come during Shakespeare's lifetime. The Shakespeare folio was an expensive book, selling for between fifteen and eighteen shillings, depending on the binding (in modern terms, from about $150 to $180). Twenty Shakespeare plays of the thirty-seven that survive first appeared in quarto, seventeen of which appeared during Shakespeare's lifetime; the rest of the plays are found only in folio.

The First Folio was published in 1623, seven years after Shakespeare's death, and was authorized by his fellow actors, the co-owners of the King's Men. This publication was certainly a mark of the company's enormous respect for Shakespeare; but it was also a way of turning the old plays, most of which were no longer current in the play-house, into ready money (the folio includes only Shake-speare's plays, not his sonnets or other nondramatic verse). Whatever the motives behind the publication of the folio, the texts it preserves constitute the basis for almost all later editions of the playwright's works. The texts, however, differ from those of the earlier quartos, sometimes in minor respects but often significantly – most strikingly in the two texts of *King Lear*, but also in important ways in *Hamlet, Othello,* and *Troilus and Cressida.* (The variants are recorded in the textual notes to each play in the new Pelican series.) The differences in these texts represent, in a sense, the essence of theater: the texts of plays were initially not intended for publication. They were scripts, designed for the actors to perform – the principal life of the play at this period was in performance. And it follows that in Shakespeare's theater the playwright typically had no say either in how his play was performed or in the disposition of his text – he was an employee of the company. The authoritative figures in the theatrical enterprise were the shareholders in the company, who were for the most part the major actors. They decided what plays were to be done; they hired the playwright and often gave him an outline of the play they wanted him to write. Often, too, the play was a collaboration: the company would retain a group of writers, and parcel out the scenes among them. The resulting script was then the property of the company, and the actors would revise it as they saw fit during the course of putting it on stage. The resulting text belonged to the company. The playwright had no rights in it once he had been paid. (This system survives largely intact in the movie industry, and most of the playwrights of Shakespeare's time were as anonymous as most screenwriters are today.) The script could also, of course, continue to change as the tastes of audiences and the requirements of the actors changed. Many – perhaps most – plays were revised when they were reintroduced after any substantial absence from the repertory, or when they were performed by a company different from the one that originally commissioned the play.

Shakespeare was an exceptional figure in this world because he was not only a shareholder and actor in his company, but also its leading playwright – he was literally his own boss. He had, moreover, little interest in the publication of his plays, and even those that appeared during his lifetime with the authorization of the company show no signs of any editorial concern on the part of the author. Theater was, for Shakespeare, a fluid and supremely responsive medium – the very opposite of the great classic canonical text that has embodied his works since 1623.

The very fluidity of the original texts, however, has meant that Shakespeare has always had to be edited. Here is an example of how problematic the editorial project inevitably is, a passage from the most famous speech in *Romeo and Juliet*, Juliet's balcony soliloquy beginning "O Romeo, Romeo, wherefore art thou Romeo?" Since the eighteenth century, the standard modern text has read,

> What's Montague? It is nor hand, nor foot,
> Nor arm, nor face, nor any other part
> Belonging to a man. O be some other name!
> What's in a name? That which we call a rose
> By any other name would smell as sweet.
>   (II.2.40-44)

Editors have three early texts of this play to work from, two quarto texts and the folio. Here is how the First Quarto (1597) reads:

> Whats *Mountague*? It is nor hand nor foote,
> Nor arme, nor face, nor any other part.
> Whats in a name? That which we call a Rose,
> By any other name would smell as sweet:

Here is the Second Quarto (1599):

> Whats *Mountague?* it is nor hand nor foote,
> Nor arme nor face, ô be some other name
> Belonging to a man.
> Whats in a name that which we call a rose,
> By any other word would smell as sweete,

And here is the First Folio (1623):

> What's *Mountague?* it is nor hand nor foote,
> Nor arme, nor face, O be some other name
> Belonging to a man.
> What? in a names that which we call a Rose,
> By any other word would smell as sweete,

There is in fact no early text that reads as our modern text does – and this is the most famous speech in the play. Instead, we have three quite different texts, all of which are clearly some version of the same speech, but none of which seems to us a final or satisfactory version. The transcendently beautiful passage in modern editions is an editorial invention: editors have succeeded in conflating and revising the three versions into something we recognize as great poetry. Is this what Shakespeare "really" wrote? Who can say? What we can say is that Shakespeare always had performance, not a book, in mind.

Books About the Shakespeare Texts

The standard study of the printing history of the First Folio is W. W. Greg, *The Shakespeare First Folio* (1955). J. K. Walton, *The Quarto Copy for the First Folio of Shakespeare* (1971), is a useful survey of the relation of the quartos to the folio. The second edition of Charlton Hinman's *Norton Facsimile* of the First Folio (1996), with a new introduction by Peter Blayney, is indispensable. Stanley Wells, Gary Taylor, John Jowett, and William Montgomery, *William Shakespeare: A Textual Companion,* keyed to the Oxford text, gives a comprehensive survey of the editorial situation for all the plays and poems.

THE GENERAL EDITORS

Introduction

THE MERRY WIVES OF WINDSOR is not a popular play –
except with theater audiences, who usually laugh themselves silly during the show and go home with the satisfaction of having had an unexpectedly jolly time. Students,
critics, and scholars have been less favorably disposed to
the comedy. It is rarely included in survey courses of
Shakespeare's works, and when mentioned at all it is likely
to be passed over with a word or two about the disap-
pointing representation of Falstaff, especially his inferiority to the character who appears in *1* and *2 Henry IV*.
Specialists have struggled with the problem of its two
texts, one much longer than the other and both uninfor-
mative and contradictory about their origins and relation
to each other. And many distinguished readers have been
unsympathetic, even hostile, to the characters and actions
that delight theatergoers. In the eighteenth century Samuel Johnson, while acknowledging the comic pleasures,
thought the structure "deficient" because "the action begins
and ends often, before the conclusion, and the different
parts might change places without inconvenience."* At the
beginning of the twentieth century A. C. Bradley identified what many consider the main difficulty, that the Falstaff of this play seems to be "an impostor": "To picture
the real Falstaff befooled like the Falstaff of the *Merry
Wives* is like imagining Iago the gull of Roderigo." As for
the comic intrigue that the faux Falstaff here attempts,

* From *Johnson on Shakespeare,* ed. Arthur Sherbo with an Introduction by
Bertrand Bronson, in *The Yale Edition of the Works of Samuel Johnson* (New
Haven: Yale University Press, 1968), VII, p. 341.

Bradley went beyond an expression of disappointment: "it is horrible."*

Although never so well known or frequently produced as *The Taming of the Shrew* or the romantic comedies, *The Merry Wives* has rarely been absent from the world's stages for long, turning up usually when producers seek an alternative to the more familiar comedies or when an aging actor possessed of enough talent and fame wants to play Falstaff. In the first half of the eighteenth century the distinguished British actor James Quin assumed the role from a young age and went on playing it some 153 times over the course of his career. Most of the great actors of the nineteenth century eagerly took the main part, although some, like the actor-manager Charles Kean, preferred to play Ford. At Stratford-upon-Avon in 1985 Bill Alexander directed a hugely popular production set in the 1950s and full of ingenious period detail: the wives, for example, received their identical letters while sitting under hair dryers in the beauty parlor. In 1990 the American actress Pat Carroll achieved attention and some critical acclaim by playing Falstaff "straight" – i.e., as if she herself were male – in Michael Kahn's production for the Shakespeare Theatre at the Folger in Washington, D.C.

The playability of *The Merry Wives* is confirmed by its popularity as a text for musical adaptation. From the beginning of the eighteenth century directors have added songs and commissioned composers, among them Sir Arthur Sullivan, to write incidental music for a new production. The poet-librettist Arrigo Boito was able to tempt the aged Giuseppe Verdi out of retirement to create *Falstaff* (1893), one of the greatest of all works in the operatic repertory. The play has attracted the theatrical intelligence of numerous talented composers from different cultures and different eras: Antonio Salieri (*Falstaff, o le tre burle*, 1799), Otto Nicolai (*Die Lustigen Weiber von*

---

* "The Rejection of Falstaff," *Oxford Lectures on Poetry* (London: Macmillan and Co., 1909), p. 248. The lectures were delivered in 1902.

Windsor, 1849), and Ralph Vaughan Williams (*Sir John in Love*, 1929). These musicians and their librettists knew a theatrical winner when they saw one, and their instincts correspond to (and probably derive from) the success of the play with audiences over the centuries.

Critical hesitation about *The Merry Wives* is no doubt related to its anomalous position in Shakespeare's oeuvre. To begin with, it is his only "English" comedy, his only work in which the comic action takes place in an explicitly native landscape. In themselves, the locales of Windsor and Frogmore, Brainford's famous tavern hostess, and the laundresses at Datchet Mead are hardly a basis for critical disapproval, but combined with the unusual subject and the uniformly ironic tone, the local setting of the play is sometimes regarded as having reduced it. Familiar places and recognizable persons do not seem to square with the dominant image, constructed and tended over four centuries, of William Shakespeare as a natural romantic, the beloved creator of enchanted forests and Bohemian sea-coasts. Ben Jonson, Thomas Middleton, or Thomas Dekker might set their satiric comedies in London and people them with city sharks and other unattractive commoners, but gentle Shakespeare is usually prized for his imaginary regions, aristocratic lovers, and providential endings.

Instead of the festivity and warmth that have become bywords of Shakespearean comedy, *The Merry Wives* presents a sequence of farcical incidents and zany secondary characters while encouraging ironic responses thought incompatible with the highest reaches of artistic ambition and achievement. The plot turns on the ridiculous consequences of foolish desire, along the way mocking sexual rapacity, greed of various sorts, marital jealousy, and several forms of male vanity. The thwarted courtship that usually fuels the engine of Shakespearean comedy is present here, but in such a subordinated, cursory form that one notices the differences from other such Shakespearean episodes, not the parallels. Moreover, the play contains more prose than any other play by Shakespeare, with verse accounting for only fifteen percent; and while *Much Ado, As You Like It,* and other popular comedies exhibit a large quotient of prose, the romantic uses of the medium in those plays make them stylistically distinct from *The Merry Wives.* In short, the play is often implicitly characterized as a kind of lapse in taste, a Shakespearean indiscretion that warrants condescension, sometimes even contempt, or (more charitably) neglect.

Seeking some means of accounting for such aberrations, editors and critics have attributed many of the play's peculiarities to the supposed circumstances of its composition. In this respect also *The Merry Wives* is unusual among Shakespeare's plays, because a legend has attached itself to the genesis of the work – the myth of royal origins. Exactly one hundred years after the appearance of the first published text, John Dennis introduced his adaptation of the comedy by declaring that the real progenitor of the original was none other than Queen Elizabeth I: "This comedy was written at her command, and by her direction, and she was so eager to see it acted that she commanded it to be finished in fourteen days."* Seven years after Dennis printed his story, Nicholas Rowe supplemented it in his early edition of Shakespeare's plays, reporting that the queen "was so well pleased with the admirable character of Falstaff in the two parts of *Henry IV* that she commanded him to continue it for one play more, and to show him in love."† The theatrical world thrives on myth and legend, and this anecdote has proved tenacious, probably because we possess so little information about Shakespeare's working habits but yearn to know how the plays came into being.

The hoary story is both specious and appealing. The

* "To the Honourable George Granville, Esq.," in *The Comical Gallant, or the Amours of Sir John Falstaff* (London: 1702), A². Further quotations from Dennis's letter and play are from this edition.
† *Some Account of the Life of Mr. William Shakespear (1709),* with an Introduction by Samuel H. Monk (The Augustan Reprint Society, n.p., 1948), pp. viii–ix.

study of Shakespeare has suffered much from such myths and stereotypes, the image of the warmhearted artist insulated from the world of commerce being one of the most damaging. In the case of this anecdote, its principal flaw is its tidiness: it is perhaps a little too comfortably tailored to our wishes and needs. It appeals first to the taste for celebrity, uniting as it does the two most famous figures of the English Renaissance in a tale about one of the world's favorite dramatic characters. More to the point, it answers to our need for an explanation of the play's perceived defects. In an introductory epistle to the printed version, Dennis justifies his adaptation on the grounds of Shakespeare's haste: "I know very well that in so short a time as this play was writ, nothing could be done that is perfect." His Prologue, spoken to the theater audience, makes a similar apology, attempting to balance reservation and admiration:

But *Shakespear's* play in fourteen days was writ,
And in that space to make all just and fit,
Was an attempt surpassing human Wit.
Yet our great *Shakespear's* matchless muse was such,
None ere in so small time performed so much.

In other words, the weaknesses in the original derive from the conditions of production, not from the master's failure. Thus readers who think Falstaff decayed, or the wordplay and foreign accents sophomoric, or the sexual intrigues simply unworthy of Britain's national poet, may cheerfully blame the requirements of the commission, consoling themselves with the belief that the dramatist was writing to order and on deadline and that probably his heart was not in his work.

And yet the convenient anecdote could just possibly be true. Its authority derives from two separate sources, distinguished literary men writing just over a century after the first performances. Chronologically, an equivalent case might be one in which an eminent writer or critic working today were to publish (or refer approvingly to) a narrative of how Joyce wrote *A Portrait of the Artist as a Young Man* or Eliot *The Waste Land.* Dennis presents the story as fact, making no effort to defend it against skepticism and invoking it to justify his new version. The Epilogue to the adaptation, apparently not by Dennis, reproduces his assumptions. That Rowe corroborated and amplified Dennis's account – rather than contradicting or doubting it – indicates that the tale must have been circulating in late Restoration and Augustan culture and that it seemed plausible to some distinguished minds in a competitive and critical age.

Some modern scholars have proposed another royal connection, arguing that *The Merry Wives* may be, or may have originated as, an occasional piece, a stage work composed in connection with the annual celebration of the Order of the Garter. On April 23, 1597, the queen and her court gathered at Westminster to honor the new members of this elite society, created by Edward III in the fourteenth century and used by subsequent monarchs to reward political friends and honor foreign dignitaries. A month after that festive evening, the installation of new members took place at Windsor, where one of the inductees was George Carey, Lord Hunsdon, then patron of Shakespeare's theatrical company. It seems reasonable that Shakespeare might have provided entertainment for the evening. Several scenes in *The Merry Wives* take place in the Garter Inn, its garrulous landlord is referred to repeatedly as "mine host of the Garter" (or, by Caius, as "de Jarteer"), and the Order of the Garter and its motto (*Honi soit qui mal y pense:* Shame to him who thinks evil) figure specifically and positively in the midnight pageant of Act V. The text of that spectacle looks as if it may have been an independent creation, a kind of masque or sketch honoring the Garter celebrants and suitable for speakers other than Parson Evans or Mistress Quickly: their language in the ceremony lacks the accents and malapropisms by which they are known in the preceding acts. And it is worth noting that the possible connection of the play with the Garter ceremony is subtly bolstered by the irrelevant coincidence that April 23 is thought to have been the playwright's birth date. But any connection between *The Merry Wives* (in whatever form) and the royal celebrations of 1597 remains unproved.

Also uncertain is the significance of some apparent topical references tenuously related to the Garter ceremony. The fourth act contains an undeveloped subplot, perhaps altered or censored between performance and publication, involving German noblemen who cheat the Host and steal his horses. Evans announces the scam by referring to the doings of some "Cozen-Garmombles," a garbled phrase ("Cozen-Iermans" in the folio text) that may allude to a small court scandal. In 1592 the German Count Mompelgard had sought membership in the Order but was put off; in 1597, the year of the supposed performance of *The Merry Wives,* he was finally offered induction (having in the meantime risen to become Count Würtemberg), but refused the honor and did not attend. Thus the joke of absconding Germans might have had resonance for those in the know. Also, some censorship may have occurred when the play made its way into print, a possibility supported by a famous textual inconsistency: in the quarto text, and apparently in the performances, Master Ford takes the assumed name of "Brooke"; but the folio text prints the name as "Broome," a change presumably made to pacify the powerful Lord Cobham, whose family name was Brooke.

Such revisions point to larger textual problems, particularly the difference between the two surviving versions. About half of Shakespeare's plays exist in more than one text – i.e., they were printed both in quarto form and in the folio of 1623. With a few notable exceptions, such as the "Bad Quarto" of *Hamlet* and the two distinct versions of *King Lear,* the differences between quarto and folio are normally minimal, resulting from slightly different manuscripts used as printer's copy, or compositors' errors, or other such mechanical explanations. But the quarto (Q) of *The Merry Wives* (1602) and the folio (F) are radically different. To mention only the most obvious differences, F contains over 1,100 more lines than Q: the scene of William's Latin lesson is absent entirely from Q; Q lacks any reference to the Garter ceremonies; and in F the Windsor residents' small-town interest in the court seems more prominent. Possibly the different published texts reflect very different source manuscripts, which further reflect very different performance versions. For example, some scholars contend that F derives from a performance given at court, probably in connection with the Garter festivities, whereas Q represents an abridged form of the play prepared specifically for the public stage (see Note on the Text). These textual tangles are related to the problem of dating the play: some scholars dispute the claim that *The Merry Wives,* or an early version of it, was performed at the 1597 Garter celebration, arguing instead that all versions of the text are later, perhaps 1599 or even 1601-2. In short, there is much about this comedy that we do not know, and many of these uncertainties have given ammunition to those unfavorably disposed to it.

Most complaints about the inferiority of *The Merry Wives* may be traced to Bradley's fundamental objection, the palpable diminution of Falstaffian wit. The title page of the 1602 quarto advertises *A Most pleasaunt and excellent conceited Comedie, of Syr Iohn Falstaffe, and the merrie Wiues of Windsor,* but almost everyone agrees that the complex rogue who dominates *Henry IV, Part One* and *Part Two,* seems much reduced. In those plays the vivacious companion of Prince Hal and sly opponent of the Lord Chief Justice is guilty of vanity, appetite, self-indulgence, and a lengthy roster of other weaknesses and crimes, but he is also shrewd, self-protective, entertaining, and ruefully aware of his own limitations. Admittedly Falstaff is vulnerable to trickery in the history plays, but there he is sufficiently charismatic not only to survive those lapses but even – except perhaps when the prince rejects him at the end of *Part Two* – to make witty capital of them. Not so in *The Merry Wives*.

The problem is not that the playwright lost his touch for characterization; rather, the contraction in Falstaff's stature is a function of the differences in dramatic mode. Comic conventions, especially in farce, tend to reduce the ridiculous victim – in this case the old fool who deserves his comeuppance – to a recognizable type who persists in his vanity. The Falstaff of the histories remains constant in his self-promotion, but at least seems to mutate as needed to protect himself, whereas in *The Merry Wives* he is duped repeatedly, and in the same way. Moreover, in the histories Falstaff's outrageous comic persona stands out against the context of politics and civil war; with that backdrop removed, he becomes less complex and less winning.

It seems inconceivable that Shakespeare was unaware of Falstaff's reduced appeal, and certain verbal turns suggest that the dramatist consciously sought to re-create some familiar zingers as a way of buoying the character. In the final scene, disguised as Herne the Hunter and wearing the stipulated horns, Falstaff comments on the absurdity of his getup and the amorous lengths to which vanity and greed have pushed him. Defending his ludicrous appearance by recalling the bestial shapes that Jove assumed to enjoy Europa and Leda, he wonders aloud, "When gods have hot backs, what shall poor men do?" (V.5.11). The analogy and the rhetorical question are reminiscent of his self-justification in Act Three of *1 Henry IV:* "Dost thou hear, Hal? Thou knowest in the state of innocency Adam fell, and what should poor Jack Falstaff do in the days of villainy?" (III.3.164-66). Likewise, some passages imply an effort to explain Falstaff's exceptional gullibility. After each escape from the Fords' house, first in the laundry basket and then disguised as the old woman of Brainford, Falstaff reflects at some length on his humiliation. Were the court to hear about the disguise as an old woman, "I warrant they would whip me with their fine wits till I were as crestfallen

as a dried pear" (IV.5.90-92), a simile that calls to mind
Falstaff's mock complaint, from the same scene in *1 Henry
IV,* that he has begun to "dwindle," that he is "withered
like an old applejohn" (III.3.2,4). As for the consequences
of his first attempt on Mrs. Ford, Falstaff acknowledges
his foolishness with rueful self-consciousness: "Have I
lived to be carried in a basket like a barrow of butcher's
offal? And to be thrown in the Thames! Well, if I be
served such another trick, I'll have my brains ta'en out,
and buttered, and give them to a dog for a New Year's
gift" (III.5.4-8). Even the harshest critics of *The Merry
Wives* can hear in that last clause something like "authen-
ticity," the multiple tones of the Falstaff they cherish. But
the passage may suggest that Shakespeare has tried, by
emphasizing and commenting on it, to forestall objec-
tions to Falstaff's repeated humiliation.

The dilation of the action into a network of intrigue implies a similar awareness that the Falstaff plot is fairly thin.
As comic theorists have been aware at least since Henri
Bergson, the mechanical repetition of an action intensifies
scornful laughter while underscoring the problem of
human fallibility, particularly the inability to change. In
making Falstaff's serial attempts on Mrs. Ford alike in
shape and result, Shakespeare devises a narrative pattern
that is common in farce, instrumental to its meaning, and
open to variation. The Falstaff schemes form the back-
bone of *The Merry Wives,* but attached to that spine are
ancillary but similar pranks involving everyone in the
cast. Two of Falstaff's retainers, Nym and Pistol, put out
with his failure to support them financially, retaliate by
betraying his designs to Masters Ford and Page. The symmetry of this disclosure – two servingmen whispering al-
ternately to two husbands about two wives – generates
complementary responses: the jealous Ford is enraged and
initiates a counterplot, while the equable Page laughs off
the threat of cuckoldry. Each is thus able to criticize the
other's reaction as inappropriate.

These parallels are supplemented by other structural

balances. Ford's scheme to expose and punish his wife's liaison with Falstaff, undertaken with the aid of the Host, is the first in a series of disguise plots – Falstaff as the old woman, the two local boys disguised as Anne Page. The Host takes delight in the symmetries of his prank for gulling the Welsh Parson Evans and the French Doctor Caius, each a "stranger," each a kind of professional, each imperfect in the English language. By arranging a duel and appointing them to meet in different spots, so that each thinks the other a coward, the schemer guarantees the men of Windsor – and the men and women in the theater – a show of verbal fireworks. As Page puts it, "I had rather hear them scold than fight" (II.1.209-10). Caius and Evans then invent a retaliatory plot against the Host involving the theft of his horses by visiting German nobles. The scheme is sketchy, perhaps a casualty of censorship or a faulty text, but apparently Shakespeare conceived of it to augment the intricacy of the action and extend the pattern of scheme and counterscheme.

Anne Page, the object of desire for three potential suitors, serves as the pivot for a series of parallel wooing plots. Her father means her to marry the idiotic Slender, her mother favors Doctor Caius, and the Host of the Garter promotes the suit of Master Fenton, the young gentleman distrusted by both parents. Each suitor engages Mistress Quickly as broker – although, in the case of the feckless Slender, Justice Shallow and others must seek her aid on his behalf. In the play's final movement the congruent schemes and parallel failures compound the ironic pleasures of the main actions. Each of the three camps arranges that Anne shall be stolen away during the Herne's Oak pageant and married hastily in the nearby village. Fenton succeeds, while Slender and Caius find themselves disappointed in identical ways:

SLENDER   I came yonder at Eton to marry Mistress Anne Page, and she's a great lubberly boy.
(V.5.178-79)

CAIUS   Vere is Mistress Page? By gar, I am cozened –
I ha' married *un garçon,* a boy; *un paysan,* by gar.
A boy, it is not Anne Page.

(V.5.198-200)

These failed elopements illuminate the central schemes involving Mistress Ford and Mistress Page, especially since all mix love and money. Falstaff, of course, is interested less in physical than in financial satisfaction: each of the wives is said to have "the rule of her husband's purse," and therefore will serve as "exchequers" to him (I.3.50 ff.). And the salient fact about Anne Page is not her virginal beauty but her wealth; in the words of Parson Evans, "Seven hundred pounds and possibilities is goot gifts" (I.1.58-59). Even Master Fenton, while claiming to have fallen in love, concedes (III.4.13-14) that the initial source of attraction was her inheritance.

The narrative model uniting these several actions is that of the trickster tricked. Stretching back at least as far as the Greek and Roman comic writers and surviving in folklore as well, such reversal plots please an audience with the delights of irony and symmetry. The pleasure is in knowing what the character does not, especially the character who thinks himself in the know or who prides himself on his acuity and superior wit. (The pronouns in the previous sentence are deliberately masculine since the self-pleased schemer is normally male.) Deviating in *The Merry Wives* from the usual mixture of irony and surprise that makes *As You Like It* or *The Merchant of Venice* so satisfying, Shakespeare trades almost exclusively in irony, furnishing the audience with information that places us in a superior epistemological position. We know what the wives know: that Falstaff doesn't know that each knows about the other's letter. We know what Ford knows: that Falstaff is after Mrs. Ford, that Falstaff does not know that Ford knows it, and that "Master Brook" is the disguised Ford. But we also know more than Ford: that his wife is faithful, that she too is scheming against Falstaff, and that after the first episode she is also actively scheming against Ford himself. Only in the revelation of the disguised boy-brides, at the very end of the play, is the audience surprised, the playwright having withheld the details of the Host's and Fenton's counterplot.

Such extensive and heavy ironies account for the more or less uniform tone of *The Merry Wives*. A masterpiece such as *Twelfth Night* derives much of its emotional power from a mixture of tones because its caustic humor and passionate poetry both complement and paradoxically amplify each other. But this farcical comedy is short on romance, deliberately so, and the love story is so marginal as to seem unimportant or perhaps even ironic itself – it may be that Fenton is a liar, and that his "love," like Falstaff's for the wives, is nothing more than greed. Because Shakespeare himself set the standard for romantic comedy – *Much Ado, As You Like It,* and *Twelfth Night* are roughly contemporaneous with *The Merry Wives* – the absence of sentiment and the abundance of scornful irony make the comic effects seem atypical. And yet these ironies are ameliorated by certain characteristic flashes of tenderness, as when Parson Evans, fearing the impending duel with Caius, attempts to cheer himself up by singing, or when Slender awkwardly tries to woo Anne Page by boasting that he has seen – and even held by the chain! – a famous London bear called Sackerson. This Shakespearean mix of poignancy and humor also sounds in Anne's response to the idea of marrying one of her parents' candidates: "Alas, I had rather be set quick i' th' earth, / And bowled to death with turnips" (III.4.84–85).

Even if we take the most cynical view of the play's genesis, regarding it as the halfhearted fulfillment of an obligation; even if we wish that Shakespeare hadn't stooped to the "base" mode of farce; even if we rank the play low on his list of achievements, we must still acknowledge and admire his gift for exploiting low comedy to generate ideas. In *The Merry Wives* he investigates the many combinations of human merit and weakness, applying his cre-

ative energy to the multifaceted topic of the human imagination. To recognize the prominence of that theme is not
to get very far in distinguishing this play from Shakespeare's other comedies, or indeed from his tragedies, histories, and tragicomedies: from the beginning to the end
of his career, the imagination is one of his favorite sub-
jects. What is distinctive in this case is the means of deliv-
ery, the particular comic form in which the playwright
represents the problem, for here he seems obsessed with
the relation between language and the mind, specifically
with the verbal medium as the expressive instrument of
imaginative talent. Speech becomes a form of action, and
given the rather conventional nature of the intrigue plot,
the delights of the play arise from Shakespeare's manipula-
tion of words rather than characters. "Action is eloquence,"
says Volumnia in *Coriolanus* (III.2.76), prompting her
inarticulate son to employ signifiers such as gesture and
bodily motion rather than words. But eloquence is also
action, as are taciturnity, stuttering, loquacity, malaprop-
ism, bluster, and the other particularized styles of speech
that beguile the ear in *The Merry Wives*.

The comedy is a showcase for verbal display, the uses of
the tongue serving as a metonymy for control of the
mind, the will, and the self in general. Falstaff's powers of
expression, of course, are the principal source of his popularity, and even if his gifts are judged to be diminished
here, his verbal wit and capacity for using words as weapons
are still considerable. The most thoroughly distinctive
speakers are Parson Evans, with his Welsh accent; Doctor
Caius, mostly shouting a barely intelligible Franglais; and
the "ranting host of the Garter" (II.1.174). The Host seems
to watch himself as he talks — "Said I well?" — and seems
compelled to repeat himself and (redundantly) to vary
every phrase: "Am I politic? am I subtle? am I a Machiavel? Shall I lose my doctor? No; he gives me the potions
and the motions. Shall I lose my parson, my priest, my Sir
Hugh? No; he gives me the proverbs and the no-verbs"
(III.1.92–96). Practically every utterance of these speakers

returns the audience explicitly to the subject of expression. The text in fact begins to look something like a prose symphony carefully orchestrated to show off the varieties, tones, and rhythms of human speech. The play calls for an exceptionally large cast, with twenty-two speaking parts, in addition to the children who take the roles of fairies in the Act Five ceremonies. And while it is Shakespeare's custom always to differentiate his speakers from one another – even in the earliest comedies – here he seems to have given particular care to such verbal distinctions.

From the opening lines the audience is confronted with the question of what things are called. In his declaration of his grievance against Falstaff (I.1.1ff.), Robert Shallow, Esquire, establishes the assorted social and legal titles he can boast. Ford's suspicion of his wife's fidelity leads him to confess a phobia about the labels and insults to which he will be subjected: "Terms! names! . . . Cuckold! Wittol! Cuckold!" (II.2.279-81). Pistol's pretentious diction, much of it borrowed from Marlovian drama, represents his ear for high-sounding terms and his taste for using a Latinate vocabulary whenever possible. For instance, in response to Nym's instructions on the rules for effective theft, Pistol corrects his partner's humble verb: " 'Convey,' the wise it call. 'Steal'? Foh, a fico for the phrase!" (I.3.27-28). Nym is enamored of fashionable jargon, using "humor" so indiscriminately that he can scarcely be understood. And the Host's impressive-sounding terms of address are invariably misapplied, from "Caesar, Keisar, and Pheazar" and "bully Hector" for Falstaff (I.3.9-11), to "Cavaliero Justice" for Shallow (as well as "Cavaliero Slender"), to "Bohemian-Tartar" for Simple, to an array of titles for Doctor Caius, including "Aesculapius," "Galen," "Castalion King Urinal," "Monsieur Mockwater," and "Hector of Greece."

This fixation on forms of expression demonstrates that "Shakespeare's English comedy" is not just a comedy set in England but a comedy explicitly about the English language – its vitality, its delights, its flexibility, and its limitations. In no other work except perhaps *Love's Labor's Lost* is the problem of language kept so insistently in the foreground. In the first act Mistress Quickly cautions that the entrance of her employer, Doctor Caius, will promise "an old abusing of God's patience and the King's English" (I.4.4-5). At the center of the play, the Host resolves to disarm Evans and Caius and relish their absurd speech: "Let them keep their limbs whole and hack our English" (III.1.70-71). In the last act, Falstaff is humiliated that he should be mocked by Evans, of all people: "Have I lived to stand at the taunt of one that makes fritters of English?" (V.5.139-40). But this concern with verbal signs extends also to the social ramifications of language. Names and words are species of a social issue, the question of establishing status and observing proper relations among persons, and this impulse manifests itself further in the class distinctions and social frictions that occupy many of the citizens: Page rejects Fenton's suit to Anne because the young man is "too great of birth" (III.4.4), "of too high a region" (III.2.65). Much is made of the misbehavior of the courtiers around Windsor and, although the subplot seems incomplete, of the aristocratic German nobles who skip out on their bill. Thus the impropriety of the Host's titles, heroic names for ignoble persons, calls attention to the gap between what things are called and what they actually are, and to proper and improper behavior among one's neighbors.

Shakespeare's fascination with the problem of naming and the literal medium from which verbal signs are composed reaches as far as single sounds. Ford as Master Brook is at pains to differentiate the pretended character (a lovesick suitor) from himself (a jealous husband), and in this role Shakespeare apparently prompts the player to lisp by giving him a festival of sibilants:

*S*ir, I hear you are a *s*cholar.
I have pur*s*ued her a*s* love ha*th* pursued me . . . and *th*at hath taught me to *s*ay *th*is,

"Love like a shadow flies when substance love
pursues;
Pursuing that that flies, and flying what pursues."

(II.2.171, 191-98)

Some say that though she appear honest to me, yet in
other places she enlargeth her mirth so far that there is
shrewd construction made of her.

(211-13).

Like words, even phonemes can be manipulated and de-
formed for comic effect.

The centrality of language to Shakespeare's comic goals
is confirmed in the scene in which Parson Evans rehearses
little Will Page in Latin, an episode irrelevant to the plot,
absent from the quarto text, and undervalued by some
critics. The boy's name is itself a nexus of conflicting and
overlapping ideas: "will" is one of the key words of the
play, "will" as desire and specifically sexual desire, as in
Shallow's double entendre asking if Slender can "carry
[his] good will" to Anne Page, or Pistol's remark that Falstaff has "studied" Mrs. Ford and "translated her will out
of honesty into English." And the schoolboy's performance
may remind us of young "Will" Shakespeare learning his
Latin from the same textbook in the Stratford grammar
school. The term "Page" figures prominently also, from
the little boy's family to the go-betweens (not only Falstaff's page, Robin, but other messengers such as Simple,
Jack Rugby, and Mistress Quickly), to the texts that get
read and "translated," to Falstaff's "love letters," those identical pages sent to the wives.

The lesson itself is a parody of a humanist exercise,
with which every Elizabethan schoolboy was familiar, re-
quiring the student to translate from Latin into English
and then back into Latin. It mimics specifically the proce-
dure and the examples of the standard sixteenth-century

textbook, Lily and Colet's *A Short Introduction of [Latin] Grammar* (published 1543). The episode is first, then, a bonus for the educated members of the audience, relying as it does on the shared experience of the schoolroom and on the standpoint of ironic superiority that Shakespeare contrives throughout the play. Untutored spectators are not excluded from the humor, however: the lesson is also an occasion for Evans's unwittingly lewd mispronunciations and Mistress Quickly's smutty misconstructions, a variation on the old theatrical trick of making children speak suggestive words they do not comprehend. But all these comic turns cohere to amplify the dramatist's comprehensive theme, the difficulty of proper interpretation, of reading and misreading texts of all kinds. Language, the system of aural signs serving as the necessary medium for communication and relation to others, is inherently limited by ambiguous sounds, the vagaries of human reception, and its vulnerability both to misconstruction and to deliberate misuse.

The lesson allows Shakespeare to exploit for humor the process of learning another language, particularly such variables as mispronunciation, faulty declensions, and contextual error:

> EVANS   . . . What is *lapis*, William?
> WILLIAM   A stone.
> EVANS   And what is "a stone," William?
> WILLIAM   A pebble.
> EVANS   No, it is *lapis*. I pray you remember in your prain.
> WILLIAM   *Lapis*.
> EVANS   That is a good William.
>
> (IV.1.28–35)

Beyond the obvious but effective shift from one register to another, in which William answers "what is 'a stone'. . . ?" as if the question were one of definition and not translation, the exchange introduces other potential misunderstandings and jokes, notably – given the bawdy undertone of the episode – the play on "stone" as testicle. Finally, it is perhaps appropriate that the transmission of Shakespeare's original text introduces a further possibility for linguistic mistake: the folio text prints William's answer as "A Peeble," which may be a simple compositor's error but which some readers construe as another genital joke, this time about urination. That the Latin lesson does nothing whatever to advance the plot is a testimony to its importance: in a play about community, about maintaining healthy relations in families and among neighbors, and about efforts to disrupt such social bonds, the scene examines the fragility of the linguistic system on which human relations depend. Community requires communication, and both are easily impaired.

The community of Windsor depends on commerce, another form of communication and exchange, and the presence of a class of working characters is one of the determinants that separates *The Merry Wives* from most of Shakespeare's other comedies. Although the various levels of early modern English society are not easily converted into twenty-first-century terms, most of the Windsor folks might be called middle-class. Falstaff's adventurism, the attempt of a social and geographical interloper to take advantage, is represented as partly a class conflict. The citizens have less in common with the aristocratic characters of the romantic comedies than with the urban gentlefolk in *The Comedy of Errors* or the Londoners in the Jacobean city comedies of the following decade. In this social sense, the play may be said to derive from the urban milieu of Plautine comedy, and it resembles Jonson's *Every Man in His Humour*, or *Epicoene*, or *The Alchemist* more than it does *Twelfth Night*.

In *The Merry Wives* money is the root of all action, or at least it motivates most of the schemes that generate comic delight. Shallow begins by charging Falstaff with a crime against his property; apparently one of Falstaff's followers has robbed Slender (not to mention Mistress Bridget,

II.2.10-11), and all three of them seem to survive by theft; the Host is concerned throughout with profit and loss. Fenton confesses to having been attracted to Anne Page initially because she is an heiress. Theoretically, at least, the patriarchal system makes Anne a matrimonial object for Page to dispose of as he wishes. Mistress Quickly accepts money from Caius, Slender, and Fenton to promote the suit of each with Anne. Falstaff, strapped for funds as always, is motivated to pursue the wives for economic, not sexual, reasons. He dismisses his hangers-on because he can't afford to maintain them, and he smugly takes money from Master Brook. Cash is the one topic that almost causes Ford's disguise to slip: "I have a bag of money here troubles me. If you will help to bear it, Sir John, take all, *or half*, for easing me of the carriage" (II.2.163-65, italics mine). And Ford is obsessed not only with money, with having his "coffers ransacked," but also with the value of his name. The term he fears most, "cuckold," signifies a husband who has lost sole possession of his spousal property.

Control – of property, of wives, and especially of words – points to the larger topic of artistic ability, the uses and misuses of the imagination. As is often the case in Shakespearean comedy, the action supplies a range of creativity, proper and improper: in *Twelfth Night*, for example, Viola's benevolent ingenuity in disguising herself and endearing herself to Orsino is juxtaposed with Malvolio's narcissistic and ill-willed designs on Olivia. Falstaff fancies himself a desirable roué, one whose status and appearance would make him attractive to the wives, and such a misconception abuses the powers of invention that also produce Falstaffian wit. His scheme to repair his purse at the expense of Ford and Page is presented as a misdirected creative act, an ill-conceived "plot" based on the ludicrous fiction of his desirability.

"Fie on sinful fantasy": the "scornful rhyme" sung by Mistress Quickly and the fairies (V.5. 92-101) in the final masque is aimed at Falstaff, but it applies generally in Windsor, especially to those who tend to think better of

themselves than they should. Other schemes reflect a similar exercise of imaginative invention – the three parallel
plots to elope with Anne Page; the Host's scheme against
Evans and Caius; and the two victims' retaliatory scheme
involving the thieving Germans. Ford's fabrication and
impersonation of the sexually frustrated Brook, a response
to his unfounded suspicions, suggest that both his jealousy and his solution to it are imaginative disorders: as
Mistress Ford says to him beforehand, "Faith, thou hast
some crotchets in thy head now" (II.1.142-43), and as
Evans remarks during the furious search of the house,
"Master Ford, you must pray, and not follow the imaginations of your own heart" (IV.2.143-44). Mistress Page
expresses to Mistress Ford the hope that their scheme will
"scrape the figures out of your husband's brains" (200-1).

The bona fide artists in the play, the creators who employ their imaginative gifts in a way that the audience is
encouraged to endorse, are, of course, the merry wives. In
imagining the plot to expose Falstaff the two women cast
themselves in conventional roles, Mistress Ford as the in-
experienced, would-be adulteress caught and shamed by
Mistress Page, her visiting neighbor. In preparation, Mistress Ford gives stage directions to the servants who act as
extras in assisting with Falstaff's escape, and the women
execute their scheme with theatrical jargon self-consciously
employed:

MRS. FORD   . . . Mistress Page, remember you your
    cue.
MRS. PAGE   I warrant thee. If I do not act it, hiss me.
                                           (III.3.32-33)

After the first escape, when Mistress Ford suggests that
her husband must have had secret intelligence of Falstaff's
visit, Mistress Page resolves to "lay a plot to try that" (170).
In this second attempt, a kind of repeat performance
arranged by giving Quickly the proper lines with which to
inveigle Falstaff back to the Fords' house, the women con-

trive his escape with the theatrical trick of disguise, dressing him as the old woman of Brainford. Moreover, when the jealous Ford enters with his gang, the women dexterously integrate him into their playlet with explicit stage business, ironically augmenting his jealousy and leading to the further punishment of Falstaff. Before the effeminized Falstaff has entered or the enraged Ford has struck a blow, Mistress Ford indirectly cues him: "Nay, good, sweet husband! Good gentlemen, let him not strike the old woman" (IV.2.166-67). The final shaming, performed at night in Windsor Park, is an extravagant theatrical "device" involving costumes, music, lighting effects, children playing fairies, and (in the elopement of Anne Page) a play within a play.

Shakespearean comedy usually invests value in its female characters: Rosalind teaches Orlando the realities of love in *As You Like It;* Hermia and Helena are absolute in their devotion to the young men in *A Midsummer Night's Dream,* who transfer their affections repeatedly. So it is in *The Merry Wives:* Shakespeare proposes a defense of female wit and spirit. As Mistress Page declares to the audience, "We'll leave a proof, by that which we will do, / Wives may be merry, and yet honest too" (IV.2.94-95). This is yet another manifestation of the larger problem of reading: vivacity should not be mistaken for promiscuity; not all fictions are dishonest; it is vital that careful discriminations be made. The wives succeed in shaming Falstaff, stimulating and thus curing Ford's unreasonable suspicions, and making their Windsor neighborhood safe and peaceful again. As usual, Shakespeare prefers the desires of young lovers to the views of their parents (and encourages his audience to do the same), so the comedy ends normatively, with the marriage of Fenton and Anne and the reconciliation of the Fords.

And yet it remains true that something seems to be missing. In *The Merry Wives* Shakespeare has not supplied the usual transformation. Normally such metamorphoses are both personal and social: people change their minds, behavior is altered, and a society is renewed or at least rescued. The touchstones for such transformations are probably *As You Like It* and *Much Ado,* but virtually all the comedies suggest some kind of beneficial reconfiguration. Even when a positive ending contains a strong countercurrent, in the person of an unaccommodated misfit, such as Shylock, Jaques, or Malvolio, the audience feels a sense of relief or even elation, as if something rare has been achieved, something vital learned. No such epiphany or sense of joy suffuses the end of *The Merry Wives.* Mistress Ford's virtue has been vindicated, Falstaff has been exposed and teased, and Anne and Fenton get what they think they want. Presumably little William will return to school tomorrow. The various disputes and frictions among the secondary characters have been resolved, at least for the moment, and the status quo has been restored. But apart from the wedding, from which the mercenary touch has never been thoroughly removed, almost nothing in Windsor has changed. Shakespeare usually prompts his audience to expect more than this. If we get the form of comedy without the spirit, the feeling of duty without enthusiasm, if we miss the customary exaltation, perhaps, in the end, the disappointment is attributable to Shakespeare's haste. Or perhaps in patching together a comedy out of the preexisting Garter entertainment he didn't have it in him. Or it may be simply that Shakespeare was stretching himself, deliberately abandoning romantic comedy for an intrigue comedy involving a favorite character and a local setting. *The Merry Wives of Windsor* may not represent his normal style, but the Shakespearean voice is audible in every episode.

RUSS MCDONALD
University of North Carolina at Greensboro

Note on the Text

THE TEXTUAL STATUS of *The Merry Wives of Windsor,* like the comedy itself, is something of an aberration in the Shakespeare canon in that two very different versions were printed in the early seventeenth century. The play first appeared in 1602 in quarto form as *A Most pleasaunt and excellent conceited Comedie, of Syr Iohn Falstaffe, and the merrie Wiues of Windsor. Entermixed with sundrie variable and pleasing humors, of Syr Hugh the Welch Knight, Iustice Shallow, and his wise Cousin M. Slender. With the swaggering vaine of Auncient Pistoll, and Corporall Nym. By William Shakespeare* (hereafter Q). It was published in the 1623 folio as *The Merry Wiues of Windsor* (hereafter F). Among the many differences are the following: F is substantially longer, some 2,730 lines to Q's 1,620; F contains the scene (IV.1) of Will Page's Latin lesson, not present in Q; the two versions of the nocturnal masque that constitutes the final scene differ significantly from each other; and Q lacks the several references to the Order of the Garter found in F (see Introduction, pp. xxxiv–xxxv). Scholars have so far been unable to offer a thorough and certain account of how these different versions came into being and how they are related to each other, although a few conclusions have been widely accepted.

Many textual scholars believe that Q was printed from a reported text known as a "memorial reconstruction," in which actors who have taken part in performances recite the play to a scribe; apparently these particular reporters had played the Host and Falstaff, since those two roles as printed in Q most closely resemble their counterparts in F. But the script these reporters provided may have been that of an abbreviated version for stage performances, perhaps by a touring company; or it may be that the version they supplied was then abbreviated for such purposes. In other words, we do not know when the Q text was cut, assuming it was, nor do we understand exactly its relation to F. In the case of *King Lear,* to take a contrary example, it seems that Shakespeare himself revised the 1608 quarto text, thus producing the version printed in the folio. With *The Merry Wives,* however, it is difficult to see one text as an authorial revision of the other. Some recent scholars have disputed the theory of memorial reconstruction, but a persuasive alternative for the state of the texts has not emerged.

F was printed from a manuscript prepared by Ralph Crane, a scribe who supplied copy for several of the folio plays. But whether this copy reflects Shakespeare's original version is unclear, if there was one "original" version. It is possible, for example, that the play began life as some kind of court entertainment associated with the Garter celebrations, and that F may be an expansion of a short urtext. Whatever its origins, F is a relatively clean text, like the others that Crane supplied for the folio. It contains few stage directions: as he often did, Crane provided what are known as "massed entries," listing at the beginning of each scene all the characters who appear in it but not giving entrances and exits with the scene. (The surviving manuscript of Middleton's *A Game at Chess,* also prepared by Crane, exhibits this scribal habit.) F also provides evidence of censorship. As in *Othello* and several other folio plays, it is clear that the manuscript has been purged of blasphemous oaths and other references to the deity, in compliance with a Parliamentary order (1606) against such language in stage plays. More interestingly, specific political pressure seems to have caused the original version to be altered. The quarto text indicates that Ford disguises himself as a character named Master Brooke (modernized in this edition to Brook). But in F "Brooke" has been changed to "Broome," probably to avoid offending the powerful Lord Cobham, whose family name was Brooke. Readers interested in pursuing these textual problems should consult Stanley Wells, Gary Taylor, John Jowett, and William Montgomery, *William Shakespeare: A Textual Companion* (Oxford: Oxford University Press, 1987); Leah Marcus, *Unediting the Renaissance: Shakespeare, Marlowe, Milton* (London: Routledge, 1996); and the Arden 3 edition of *The Merry Wives of Windsor,* ed. Giorgio Melchiori (London: Thomas Nelson, 2000).

The present edition follows F closely, although "Brook" has been reinstated and oaths have been restored with the help of Q: for example, Evans's "'Pless my soul" (F) becomes, with the help of Q, "Jeshu pless my soul" (III.1.11). In a few other instances Q is helpful in providing a line or word that seems necessary but is not present in F. Stage directions from Q have also been added, as well as others that are obviously necessary: all such material is here printed in brackets. Thus *[Enter] Mistress Ford* at II.1.29 indicates that the name "Mistress Ford" has been moved from the beginning of the scene in F to the line where she enters. Caius's English is limited and mispronounced for humor; his native French, however, would presumably be spoken correctly, and thus I follow other editors in adjusting F's irregular transcription of certain words and phrases.

The following list registers those cases in which the folio text has been emended. Printed in italics is the reading adopted here; the parentheses contain the source of the change, usually Q but sometimes the name of an earlier editor; the folio reading is in roman. Obvious typographical errors and turned letters are not listed.

I.1 25 *py'r Lady* (Capell) per-lady 41 *George* (Theobald) Thomas 56 *SHALLOW* (Capell) Slender 233 *faul'* (Hanmer) fall
I.3 14 *lime* (Q) liue 47 *well . . . will* (White) will . . . will 51 *legion* (Q: legians) legend 77 *titely* (Q) tightly 80 *o' the* (F2: oth') ith' 81 *humor* (Q) honor 92 *Page* (Q) Ford 93 *Ford* (Q) Page 97 *Page* (Malone) Ford
I.4 41 *une boîte en vert* (Craik) vnboyteene verd 81 *baille* (Cambridge) ballow
II.1 1 *I* (F2) not in F 52 *praised* (Theobald) praise 57 *Hundredth Psalm* (Rowe) hundred Psalms 125-26 *and there's the humor of it* (Q) not in F 194 *FORD* (Q3) Shallow 199 *asniers* (this edition) An-heires
II.2 21 *I, ay, I* (White) I, I, I 22 *God* (Q) heauen 49 *God* (Q) heauen

53 *God* (Hibbard) heauen   136 etc. *Brook* (Q: Brooke) Broome   254
cuckoldy (Q3) cuckoldly   258 *cuckoldy* cuckoldly   290 *God* (Q) Heauen
II.3 16 *God bless* (Q) 'Blesse   17 *God save* (Q) 'Saue   51 *word* (Q) not in
F   58 *titely* (Q) tightly
III.1 11 *Jeshu pless* (Q) 'Plesse   39 *God save* (Q) 'Saue   40 *God pless* (Q)
'Plesse   80 *By Jeshu* (Q) not in F   81–82 *for missing your meetings and
appointments* (Q) not in F   96–97 *Give me thy hand, terrestrial; so* (Q)
not in F   101 *lads* (Q) Lad   103 *Afore God* (Q) Trust me
III.3 3 *Robert* (Bowers) Robin   54 *By the Lord* (Collier, adapting Q) not in
F   161 *what* (Harness) who
III.4 12 FENTON (F2) not in F   57 *God* (Q) Heauen
III.5 8 *'Sblood* (Q) not in F   55 *By the mass* (Q) Oh   56 *God save* (Q)
Blesse   82 *By the Lord* (Q) Yes
IV.1 1 *Mistress* (Oxford) M.   31 *pebble* Peeble   43 *hung* (Pope) hing   55
Genitivo (Singer) Genitiue   63 *lunatics* (Capell) Lunaties   71 *quae*
(Pope) que   72 *quae*'s (Pope) Ques
IV.2 18 *lunes* (Theobald) lines   50 MRS. PAGE (Malone) not in F   58 MRS.
PAGE (Malone) Mrs. Ford   93 *him* (F2) not in F   104 *as lief* (F2) liefe as
107–8 *villains* (Collier) villaine   109 *gang* (F2: ging) gin   122 *God*
(Oxford, adapting Q) Heauen   167 *not* (F2) not in F   178 *Jeshu* (Q)
yea, and no
IV.3 9 *house* (Q) houses
IV.4 7 *cold* (Rowe) gold   26 *Herne* (Q) Horne   31 *makes* (F2) make   41
Disguised like Herne, with huge horns on his head (from Q, with *Herne* for
"Horne") not in F   59 MRS. FORD (Rowe) Ford
IV.5 40 SIMPLE (Rowe) Falstaff   50 *Sir Tyke* (Q) Sir: like   71 *Cozen-
Garmombles* (Q) Cozen-Iermans   72 *Readings* (Q) Readins
V.3 12 *Hugh* (Capell) Herne
V.5 109 *cuckoldy* cuckoldly   191 *white* (Rowe) greene   195 *green* (Rowe)
white   201 *green* (Pope) white

The Merry Wives
of Windsor

[NAMES OF THE ACTORS

SIR JOHN FALSTAFF

ALICE FORD *the merry wives*
MEG PAGE

FRANK FORD *their husbands*
GEORGE PAGE

ANNE PAGE, *the Pages' daughter*
MASTER FENTON, *her suitor, a gentleman*
WILLIAM PAGE, *the Pages' young son*
MISTRESS QUICKLY, *housekeeper for Doctor Caius*
SIR HUGH EVANS, *a Welsh parson*
DOCTOR CAIUS, *a French physician*
HOST OF THE GARTER, *an innkeeper at Windsor*
ROBERT SHALLOW, *a visiting justice of the peace*
ABRAHAM SLENDER, *his kinsman*
PETER SIMPLE, *servant to Slender*

BARDOLPH
PISTOL *followers of Falstaff*
NYM

ROBIN, *a boy, page to Falstaff*
JOHN RUGBY, *servant to Doctor Caius*

ROBERT *servants to the Fords*
JOHN

SCENE: *In and around the town of Windsor*]

*

The Merry Wives
of Windsor

❧ **I.1** *Enter Justice Shallow, Slender, [and] Sir Hugh Evans.*

SHALLOW Sir Hugh, persuade me not; I will make a Star 1
Chamber matter of it. If he were twenty Sir John Fal-
staffs he shall not abuse Robert Shallow, Esquire. 3
SLENDER In the county of Gloucester, Justice of Peace
and Coram. 5
SHALLOW Ay, cousin Slender, and Custalorum. 6
SLENDER Ay, and Ratolorum too; and a gentleman 7
born, Master Parson, who writes himself Armigero, in 8
any bill, warrant, quittance, or obligation – Armigero! 9
SHALLOW Ay, that I do, and have done any time these 10
three hundred years.

I.1 Before the Pages' house in Windsor **1–2** *Star Chamber* (Elizabethan high court, named for its meeting room in the palace of Westminster, with stars painted on the ceiling) **3** *Esquire* (title for a gentleman) **5** *Coram* (common term for "quorum," designating a member of the bench) **6** *cousin* (a term for any kinsman; Slender is Shallow's nephew or grand-nephew); *Custalorum* i.e., Custos Rotulorum, keeper of the judicial rolls or archives, an important office **7** *Ratolorum* (mistake for Rotulorum) **8** *Armigero* Esquire (Latin) **9** *bill . . . obligation* (legal documents: a *bill* is an early bank draft, *warrant* a pledge or authorization, *quittance* a receipt, *obligation* a contract or agreement)

12 SLENDER   All his successors gone before him hath done't,
      and all his ancestors that come after him may. They
14   may give the dozen white luces in their coat.
    SHALLOW   It is an old coat.
16 EVANS   The dozen white louses do become an old coat
17   well. It agrees well, passant; it is a familiar beast to man,
      and signifies love.
19 SHALLOW   The luce is the fresh fish. The salt fish is an
20   old coat.
21 SLENDER   I may quarter, coz?
    SHALLOW   You may, by marrying.
    EVANS   It is marring indeed, if he quarter it.
    SHALLOW   Not a whit.
25 EVANS   Yes, py'r Lady. If he has a quarter of your coat,
26   there is but three skirts for yourself, in my simple con-
27   jectures. But that is all one. If Sir John Falstaff have
      committed disparagements unto you, I am of the
      church, and will be glad to do my benevolence to make
30   atonements and compromises between you.
31 SHALLOW   The Council shall hear it. It is a riot.
32 EVANS   It is not meet the Council hear a riot. There is no
      fear of Got in a riot. The Council, look you, shall desire

---

12–13 *successors . . . ancestors* (Slender reverses the meaning of the two
nouns)   14 *may give . . . coat* are entitled to display impressive symbols in
their coat of arms (in heraldry, *give* = display or present); *luces* pike – i.e., fish
(may glance mockingly at Sir Thomas Lucy, of Charlecote near Stratford,
whose arms displayed three luces)   16 *louses* (Evans's mistake for *luces* – the
first of the Welshman's many humorous mispronunciations)   17 *well, passant* passing well, extremely well (but *passant* is a term from heraldry signify-
ing a "walking" animal); *familiar* domestic   19–20 *luce . . . coat* (the joke
here, apparently involving a pun on *coat* and "cod," a salt fish, has not been
satisfactorily explained; the text may be corrupt)   21 *quarter* combine arms
of two families (in ll. 25 ff., Evans takes *quarter* literally, in reference to the
coat); *coz* cousin (like "kinsman," a general term for a family member)   25
py'r Lady i.e., by our Lady (the Virgin Mary – like *Marry* in l. 116, a mild
oath; Evans's stage Welsh accent converts initial *b* into *p* [*by* becomes *py*],
pronounces *v* as *f* and *d* as *t* [as in *Fery goot*], and omits initial *w* ['oman for
woman])   26 *three skirts* (referring to a long coat that had four taillike
panels – hence the joke on *quarter*)   27 *all one* all the same (i.e., "never
mind")   31 *Council* Privy Council, sitting in the *Star Chamber*, ll. 1–2; *riot*
disturbance of the peace   32 *meet* appropriate (Evans mistakes *Council* for a
church council, without jurisdiction on riots)

to hear the fear of Got, and not to hear a riot. Take   34
your vizaments in that.

SHALLOW   Ha! O' my life, if I were young again, the
sword should end it.

EVANS   It is petter that friends is the sword, and end it –   38
and there is also another device in my prain, which per-
adventure prings goot discretions with it. There is   40
Anne Page, which is daughter to Master George Page,
which is pretty virginity.

SLENDER   Mistress Anne Page? She has brown hair, and
speaks small like a woman.   44

EVANS   It is that fery person for all the 'orld, as just as
you will desire. And seven hundred pounds of moneys,
and gold and silver, is her grandsire, upon his death's
bed – Got deliver to a joyful resurrections – give, when
she is able to overtake seventeen years old. It were a
goot motion if we leave our pribbles and prabbles, and   50
desire a marriage between Master Abraham and Mis-   51
tress Anne Page.

SLENDER   Did her grandsire leave her seven hundred
pound?

EVANS   Ay, and her father is make her a petter penny.   55

SHALLOW   I know the young gentlewoman. She has good
gifts.   57

EVANS   Seven hundred pounds and possibilities is goot   58
gifts.

SHALLOW   Well, let us see honest Master Page. Is Falstaff   60
there?

EVANS   Shall I tell you a lie? I do despise a liar as I do despise one that is false, or as I despise one that is not

---

34–35 *Take . . . that* i.e., think about that (*vizaments* = advisements)   38
that . . . it that friends should be the means of bringing about the end   44
small i.e., in a low, delicate voice   50 *goot motion* good suggestion; *pribbles
and prabbles* (perhaps "quibbles" and "brabbles" [squabbles] – i.e., trivial
disputes)   51–52 *Mistress* (the title could signify a married or an unmarried
woman; the modern sexual sense does not apply)   55 *a petter penny* i.e., still
more money ("better penny" was a proverbial phrase)   57 *gifts* qualities, talents   58 *possibilities* prospects

true. The knight Sir John is there; and, I beseech you,
be ruled by your well-willers. I will peat the door for
Master Page. *[Knocks.]* What ho! Got pless your house
here.

PAGE   *[Within]* Who's there?
        [Enter] Master Page.

EVANS   Here is Got's plessing, and your friend, and Jus-
70   tice Shallow; and here young Master Slender, that per-
71   adventures shall tell you another tale, if matters grow to
     your likings.

73 PAGE   I am glad to see your worships well. I thank you
     for my venison, Master Shallow.

SHALLOW   Master Page, I am glad to see you. Much good
     do it your good heart! I wished your venison better – it
77   was ill killed. How doth good Mistress Page? And I
     thank you always with my heart, la; with my heart.

PAGE   Sir, I thank you.

80 SHALLOW   Sir, I thank you; by yea and no, I do.

PAGE   I am glad to see you, good Master Slender.

82 SLENDER   How does your fallow greyhound, sir? I heard
83   say he was outrun on Cotsall.

PAGE   It could not be judged, sir.

SLENDER   You'll not confess, you'll not confess.

86 SHALLOW   That he will not – 'tis your fault, 'tis your
     fault. 'Tis a good dog.

88 PAGE   A cur, sir.

SHALLOW   Sir, he's a good dog, and a fair dog. Can there
90   be more said? He is good and fair. Is Sir John Falstaff
     here?

92 PAGE   Sir, he is within. And I would I could do a good
     office between you.

---

71 *tell . . . tale* have more to say (proverbial phrase) 73 *your worships* you
gentlemen (a polite term of address) 77 *ill killed* (perhaps the deer shot ille-
gally by Falstaff; see below, ll. 104–8) 82 *fallow* fawn-colored 83 *on Cotsall* i.e., in races held on the Cotswold hills in Gloucestershire 86 *That . . .
fault* i.e., Page won't admit (*confess*) it, and you (Slender) are to blame for
teasing him 88 *A cur* an ordinary dog, nothing special 92–93 *good office*
good turn (i.e., mediate)

EVANS   It is spoke as a Christians ought to speak.

SHALLOW   He hath wronged me, Master Page.

PAGE   Sir, he doth in some sort confess it.

SHALLOW   If it be confessed, it is not redressed. Is not   97
that so, Master Page? He hath wronged me; indeed, he
hath. At a word, he hath, believe me. Robert Shallow,
Esquire, saith he is wronged.   100

PAGE   Here comes Sir John.

   [Enter Sir John] Falstaff, Bardolph, Nym, [and] Pistol.

FALSTAFF   Now, Master Shallow, you'll complain of me
to the king?

SHALLOW   Knight, you have beaten my men, killed my
deer, and broke open my lodge.   105

FALSTAFF   But not kissed your keeper's daughter?

SHALLOW   Tut, a pin! This shall be answered.   107

FALSTAFF   I will answer it straight – I have done all this.   108
That is now answered.

SHALLOW   The Council shall know this.   110

FALSTAFF   'Twere better for you if it were known in coun-   111
sel: you'll be laughed at.

EVANS   *Pauca verba,* Sir John; good worts.   113

FALSTAFF   Good worts? good cabbage! Slender, I broke   114
your head. What matter have you against me?   115

SLENDER   Marry, sir, I have matter in my head against   116
you, and against your cony-catching rascals, Bardolph,   117
Nym, and Pistol.

BARDOLPH   You Banbury cheese!   119

SLENDER   Ay, it is no matter.   120

---

97 *If . . . redressed* i.e., even if he admits it, that's not enough (proverb: "Confession of a fault is half amends")   105 *lodge* gamekeeper's house in a park or forest   107 *pin* trifle; *answered* redressed, accounted for   108 *straight* straightaway, immediately (with a pun on "strait," strictly)   111–12 *in counsel* privately, not publicly   113 *Pauca verba* few words (Latin)   114 *cabbage* (Falstaff plays on Evans's mispronunciation of "words," construing it as *worts,* the general term for any cabbagelike plant); *broke* injured by breaking the skin   115 *matter* complaint, legal issue   116 *Marry* by the Virgin Mary (a mild oath)   117 *cony-catching rascals* con men (*cony* = rabbit, a metaphor for the sucker in a con game)   119 *Banbury cheese* i.e., very thin (proverbial)   120 *it . . . matter* i.e., never mind

121 PISTOL   How now, Mephostophilus!

SLENDER   Ay, it is no matter.

123 NYM   Slice, I say! *Pauca, pauca.* Slice! that's my humor.

124 SLENDER   Where's Simple, my man? Can you tell,
cousin?

EVANS   Peace, I pray you. Now let us understand. There
is three umpires in this matter, as I understand; that is
128 Master Page, fidelicet, Master Page; and there is myself,
fidelicet, myself; and the three party is, lastly and fi-
130 nally, mine host of the Garter.

PAGE   We three to hear it and end it between them.

EVANS   Fery goot. I will make a prief of it in my note-
book, and we will afterwards 'ork upon the cause with
as great discreetly as we can.

FALSTAFF   Pistol.

PISTOL   He hears with ears.

137 EVANS   The tevil and his tam! What phrase is this, "He
hears with ear"? Why, it is affectations.

FALSTAFF   Pistol, did you pick Master Slender's purse?

140 SLENDER   Ay, by these gloves, did he – or I would I
141 might never come in mine own great chamber again
142 else – of seven groats in mill sixpences, and two Edward
shovelboards, that cost me two shilling and twopence
144 apiece of Yed Miller, by these gloves.

FALSTAFF   Is this true, Pistol?

---

121 *Mephostophilus* (devil's name from Marlowe's *Doctor Faustus*, c. 1592;
Pistol characteristically quotes – misquotes – heroic or tragic verse) 123
Slice i.e., abbreviate, cut things short; *that's my humor* (Nym's catchword,
humor, used obsessively throughout, meant mainly "mood" or "temperament" c. 1600, but also "fashion," "idea," "notion," or, most frequently, "expression," "way of thinking about it") 124 *man* manservant 128 *fidelicet*
i.e., videlicet, namely 130 *Garter* (the name of the inn may suggest the celebration of the Order of the Garter at Windsor, for which a version of *Merry
Wives* may have been performed; see Introduction, pp. xxxiv–xxxv) 137 *The
tevil . . . tam* i.e., "the devil and his dam [mother]," a popular phrase 141
great chamber (largest room in a house) 142 *seven groats* twenty-eight pence
(a *groat* was worth fourpence); *mill sixpences* machine-made coins (Slender's
arithmetic seems confused: twenty-eight pence is not divisible by six) 142–
43 *Edward shovelboards* discarded shillings from the reign of Edward VI,
used in the game of shovelboard 144 *Yed* (nickname for "Edward")

EVANS   No, it is false, if it is a pickpurse.

PISTOL

Ha, thou mountain foreigner! Sir John and master 147
mine,

I combat challenge of this latten bilbo. 148

Word of denial in thy *labras* here! 149

Word of denial! Froth and scum, thou liest. 150

SLENDER   By these gloves, then 'twas he.

NYM   Be avised, sir, and pass good humors. I will say
"marry trap" with you, if you run the nuthook's humor 153
on me. That is the very note of it. 154

SLENDER   By this hat, then he in the red face had it; for 155
though I cannot remember what I did when you made
me drunk, yet I am not altogether an ass.

FALSTAFF   What say you, Scarlet and John? 158

BARDOLPH   Why, sir, for my part, I say the gentleman
had drunk himself out of his five sentences. *160*

EVANS   It is his "five senses." Fie, what the ignorance is. 161

BARDOLPH   And being fap, sir, was, as they say, cashiered; 162
and so conclusions passed the careers. 163

SLENDER   Ay, you spake in Latin then too. But 'tis no
matter. I'll ne'er be drunk whilst I live again, but in
honest, civil, godly company, for this trick. If I be
drunk, I'll be drunk with those that have the fear of
God, and not with drunken knaves.

---

147 *mountain foreigner* i.e., Welshman (Wales was famous for its mountains)
148 *latten bilbo* sword, originally from Bilbao (again mocking the skinny
Slender)   149 *labras* lips (faulty Latin or Italian)   150 *Froth and scum* (insult referring to the worthless head and dregs of a drink)   153 *"marry trap"*
with you (an unclear insult, perhaps referring to the children's game of trap-
ball – i.e., "run along and play"); *run the nuthook's humor* i.e., call a constable
(*nuthook*, a long pole for hooking branches, became slang for "officer")   154
very note fact   155 *he . . . face* i.e., Bardolph, whose complexion is noticeably
red (see I.3.23 n. and Shakespeare's *1* and *2 Henry IV* and *Henry V*)   158
Scarlet and John (Robin Hood's companions – i.e., Bardolph and Pistol, with
another allusion to Bardolph's face)   161 *Fie* (strong expression of disgust)
162 *fap* drunk; *cashiered* relieved of cash, robbed (wordplay: to *cashier* means to
relieve someone of duty, to dismiss)   163 *conclusions . . . careers* i.e., one thing
quickly led to another (in horsemanship, *career* = a short gallop at full speed)

169 EVANS   So Got 'udge me, that is a virtuous mind.
170 FALSTAFF   You hear all these matters denied, gentlemen.
You hear it.
*[Enter] Anne Page [with wine], Mistress Ford, [and]
Mistress Page.*
PAGE   Nay, daughter, carry the wine in; we'll drink
within.   *[Exit Anne Page.]*
SLENDER   O heaven, this is Mistress Anne Page.
PAGE   How now, Mistress Ford?
176 FALSTAFF   Mistress Ford, by my troth, you are very well
177 met. By your leave, good mistress.
[Kisses her.]
PAGE   Wife, bid these gentlemen welcome. Come, we
179 have a hot venison pasty to dinner. Come, gentlemen, I
180 hope we shall drink down all unkindness.
[Exeunt all but Shallow, Slender, and Evans.]
SLENDER   I had rather than forty shillings I had my book
182 of *Songs and Sonnets* here.
[Enter] Simple.
How now, Simple; where have you been? I must wait
184 on myself, must I? You have not the *Book of Riddles*
about you, have you?
SIMPLE   *Book of Riddles?* Why, did you not lend it to
187 Alice Shortcake upon Allhallowmas last, a fortnight
188 afore Michaelmas?
SHALLOW   Come, coz, come, coz; we stay for you. A
190 word with you, coz. Marry, this, coz – there is as 'twere

---

169 *'udge* i.e., judge   176 *by my troth* (mild oath: *troth* = truth)   177 *By your leave* (expression of courtesy; here "Let me kiss you in greeting")   179 *pasty* meat pie; *dinner* (here the midday meal)   182 *Songs and Sonnets* (also known as *Tottel's Miscellany,* published 1557, a popular collection of love poetry and other verse)   184 *Book of Riddles* (not specifically identified, although several joke books were published in the sixteenth century)   187 *Allhallowmas* All Saints' Day, November 1   188 *Michaelmas* Saint Michael's Day, September 29 (Simple seems confused, since Michaelmas is a month before All Saints' Day)

a tender, a kind of tender, made afar off by Sir Hugh   191
here. Do you understand me?   192

SLENDER Ay, sir, you shall find me reasonable. If it be so,
I shall do that that is reason.

SHALLOW Nay, but understand me.

SLENDER So I do, sir.

EVANS Give ear to his motions. Master Slender, I will
description the matter to you, if you be capacity of it.

SLENDER · Nay, I will do as my cousin Shallow says — I
pray you pardon me. He's a justice of peace in his coun-   200
try, simple though I stand here.   201

EVANS But that is not the question. The question is concerning your marriage.

SHALLOW Ay, there's the point, sir.

EVANS Marry, is it, the very point of it, to Mistress Anne
Page.

SLENDER Why, if it be so, I will marry her upon any reasonable demands.

EVANS But can you affection the 'oman? Let us command to know that of your mouth, or of your lips — for   210
divers philosophers hold that the lips is parcel of the   211
mouth. Therefore, precisely, can you carry your good   212
will to the maid?

SHALLOW Cousin Abraham Slender, can you love her?

SLENDER I hope, sir, I will do as it shall become one that
would do reason.

EVANS Nay, Got's lords and his ladies! you must speak
possitable, if you can carry her your desires towards her.   218

SHALLOW That you must. Will you, upon good dowry,   219
marry her?   220

---

191 *a tender* an offer; *afar off* obliquely, not obviously 192 *understand me*
(from here through l. 201 Slender misunderstands the marriage *tender*,
thinking it an offer to settle the Shallow-Falstaff dispute) 201 *simple . . .
here* i.e., I may not be very bright, but I know what's what (there may be
some byplay here with his servant "Simple") 211 *divers* various; *parcel* part
212–13 *carry . . . will* (double entendre, *will* being a slang term for the genitals) 218 *possitable* i.e., positively, fervently 219 *upon good dowry* i.e., with
a proper monetary settlement from her father

SLENDER   I will do a greater thing than that upon your request, cousin, in any reason.

223 SHALLOW   Nay, conceive me, conceive me, sweet coz: what I do is to pleasure you, coz. Can you love the maid?

SLENDER   I will marry her, sir, at your request; but if there be no great love in the beginning, yet heaven may decrease it upon better acquaintance when we are married and have more occasion to know one another. I

230 hope upon familiarity will grow more content. But if you say, "Marry her," I will marry her; that I am freely dissolved, and dissolutely.

EVANS   It is a fery discretion answer, save the faul' is in the 'ord "dissolutely": the 'ort is, according to our meaning, "resolutely." His meaning is good.

SHALLOW   Ay, I think my cousin meant well.

SLENDER   Ay, or else I would I might be hanged, la.
   [Enter Anne Page.]

SHALLOW   Here comes fair Mistress Anne. Would I were young for your sake, Mistress Anne.

240 ANNE   The dinner is on the table. My father desires your worships' company.

242 SHALLOW   I will wait on him, fair Mistress Anne.

243 EVANS   'Od's plessed will! I will not be absence at the grace.   *[Exeunt Shallow and Evans.]*

ANNE   Will't please your worship to come in, sir?

SLENDER   No, I thank you, forsooth, heartily – I am very well.

ANNE   The dinner attends you, sir.

249 SLENDER   I am not a-hungry, I thank you forsooth. *[To*
250   *Simple]* Go, sirrah, for all you are my man, go wait

---

223 *conceive me* make sure you understand me   230 *content* (alluding to the proverb "Familiarity breeds contempt"; some editors emend *content* to "contempt," but the joke is clear in either case)   242 *wait on him* join him (i.e., accept the invitation)   243 *'Od's* (an abbreviated or euphemistic form of "God's," which came into being in the late sixteenth century as a means of avoiding blasphemy; cf. the modern "gosh")   249 *forsooth* in truth (another gentle oath)   250 *sirrah* (term of address to a servant or one of lower station, as at IV.2.125)

upon my cousin Shallow. *[Exit Simple.]* A justice of
peace sometime may be beholding to his friend for a
man. I keep but three men and a boy yet, till my   253
mother be dead. But what though? Yet I live like a poor   254
gentleman born.

ANNE   I may not go in without your worship: they will
not sit till you come.

SLENDER   I' faith, I'll eat nothing. I thank you as much   258
as though I did.

ANNE   I pray you, sir, walk in.   260

SLENDER   I had rather walk here, I thank you. I bruised
my shin th' other day with playing at sword and dagger
with a master of fence – three veneys for a dish of   263
stewed prunes – and, by my troth, I cannot abide the   264
smell of hot meat since. Why do your dogs bark so? Be 265
there bears i' the town?

ANNE   I think there are, sir; I heard them talked of.

SLENDER   I love the sport well, but I shall as soon quarrel   268
at it as any man in England. You are afraid if you see
the bear loose, are you not?   270

ANNE   Ay indeed, sir.

SLENDER   That's meat and drink to me, now. I have seen
Sackerson loose twenty times, and have taken him by   273
the chain; but, I warrant you, the women have so cried
and shrieked at it, that it passed. But women, indeed, 275
cannot abide 'em; they are very ill-favored rough things.   276
[Enter Page.]

PAGE   Come, gentle Master Slender, come. We stay for
you.

253–54 *I . . . dead* i.e., my retinue is relatively small until I come into my fortune   254 *what though* i.e., so what   258 *I' faith* i.e., in faith, truly (another
mild oath)   263 *fence* fencing; *veneys* bouts   264 *stewed prunes* (associated
with brothels, known as "stews"; Slender seems to have been fighting over a
whore)   265 *hot meat* any solid food (again with sexual undertones)   268
the sport bearbaiting, in which dogs attack staked bears   273 *Sackerson* a famous bear in London in the 1590s   275 *passed* surpassed belief (Page uses a
similar expression at IV.2.113, 126)   276 *ill-favored* ugly

SLENDER   I'll eat nothing, I thank you, sir.

280 PAGE   By cock and pie, you shall not choose, sir! Come, come.

SLENDER   Nay, pray you lead the way.

PAGE   Come on, sir.

SLENDER   Mistress Anne, yourself shall go first.

ANNE   Not I, sir; pray you keep on.

SLENDER   Truly, I will not go first; truly, la. I will not do you that wrong.

ANNE   I pray you, sir.

SLENDER   I'll rather be unmannerly than troublesome.
290   You do yourself wrong, indeed, la.   *Exeunt.*

*

∾ **I.2** *Enter Evans and Simple.*

1 EVANS   Go your ways, and ask of Doctor Caius' house, which is the way; and there dwells one Mistress
3   Quickly, which is in the manner of his nurse, or his dry nurse, or his cook, or his laundry, his washer, and his wringer.

SIMPLE   Well, sir.

EVANS   Nay, it is petter yet. Give her this letter, for it is a
8   'oman that altogether's acquaintance with Mistress Anne Page; and the letter is to desire and require her to
10   solicit your master's desires to Mistress Anne Page. I pray you be gone. I will make an end of my dinner –
12   there's pippins and cheese to come.   *Exeunt.*

*

---

280 *cock and pie* (a mild, jocular oath of uncertain origin; *cock* is probably a corruption of "God")
   I.2 Before the Pages' house 1 *Go your ways* (colloquial preface – i.e., "get along and . . ."); *ask of* inquire about; *Caius* (now usually pronounced "Kī-us"; in the sixteenth century probably "Kā-us") 3–4 *dry nurse* attendant or housekeeper (as opposed to an infant's wet nurse) 8 *altogether's acquaintance* is thoroughly acquainted 12 *pippins* apples; *cheese* (stage Welshmen were conventionally fond of cheese)

∾ **I.3** *Enter Falstaff, Host, Bardolph, Nym, Pistol,*
[and Robin, Falstaff's] Page.

FALSTAFF   Mine host of the Garter.

HOST   What says my bullyrook? Speak scholarly and   2
wisely.

FALSTAFF   Truly, mine host, I must turn away some of   4
my followers.

HOST   Discard, bully Hercules, cashier. Let them wag;   6
trot, trot.

FALSTAFF   I sit at ten pounds a week.   8

HOST   Thou'rt an emperor – Caesar, Keisar, and Pheazar.   9
I will entertain Bardolph: he shall draw, he shall tap.   10
Said I well, bully Hector?   11

FALSTAFF   Do so, good mine host.

HOST   I have spoke; let him follow. *[To Bardolph]* Let me
see thee froth and lime. I am at a word; follow. *[Exit.]*   14

FALSTAFF   Bardolph, follow him. A tapster is a good
trade. An old cloak makes a new jerkin; a withered   16
servingman, a fresh tapster. Go, adieu.

BARDOLPH   It is a life that I have desired. I will thrive.

PISTOL   O base Hungarian wight! Wilt thou the spigot   19
wield?   *[Exit Bardolph.]*   20

NYM   He was gotten in drink. Is not the humor con-   21
ceited?

I.3 A room in the Garter Inn   2 *bullyrook* fine fellow, boon companion   4–5
turn . . . followers dismiss some of my attendants   6 *cashier* fire, dismiss; *wag*
(1) go it alone, (2) be hanged   8 *sit at* must pay, am charged   9 *Keisar* kaiser,
emperor; *Pheazar* (perhaps "visier" – i.e., Turkish viceroy – but chiefly a
high-sounding title rhyming with the first two)   10 *entertain . . . tap* employ Bardolph as bartender, who will draw beer and tap kegs   11 *Hector* Trojan hero (like *Hercules* in l. 6, one of the Host's inappropriate names for
Falstaff)   14 *froth and lime* cheat customers by (1) giving them large foam
heads on glasses of beer, (2) putting lime into stale or inferior beer to disguise
the bad taste; *am at a word* will be brief   16 *jerkin* jacket   19 *Hungarian
wight* i.e., down-and-out fellow (play on "hungry")   21 *gotten in drink* conceived ("begotten") by drunken parents, and therefore fit for the job of tapster   21–22 *conceited* ingenious, clever

23 FALSTAFF   I am glad I am so acquit of this tinderbox. His
thefts were too open. His filching was like an unskillful
25 singer: he kept not time.
26 NYM   The good humor is to steal at a minute's rest.
27 PISTOL   "Convey," the wise it call. "Steal"? Foh, a fico for
the phrase!
29 FALSTAFF   Well, sirs, I am almost out at heels.
30 PISTOL   Why then, let kibes ensue.
31 FALSTAFF   There is no remedy – I must cony-catch, I
32 must shift.
PISTOL   Young ravens must have food.
FALSTAFF   Which of you know Ford of this town?
35 PISTOL   I ken the wight. He is of substance good.
FALSTAFF   My honest lads, I will tell you what I am
about.
38 PISTOL   Two yards, and more.
FALSTAFF   No quips now, Pistol. Indeed, I am in the
40 waist two yards about – but I am now about no waste;
41 I am about thrift. Briefly, I do mean to make love to
42 Ford's wife. I spy entertainment in her: she discourses,
43 she carves, she gives the leer of invitation. I can con-
44 strue the action of her familiar style; and the hardest

---

23 *acquit* rid; *tinderbox* container for flammable materials, an early version of
a matchbox – alluding to (1) Bardolph's red face, (2) his fiery temper   25
kept not time i.e., stole at the wrong times   26 *good humor* (here probably
"trick of it"); *minute's rest* i.e., quickly, between notes (playing on Falstaff's
musical simile)   27 *fico* fig (Italian; but also an expletive with obscene hand
gesture)   29 *out at heels* i.e., broke (with worn-out shoes)   30 *kibes* sores, especially on the feet   31 *cony-catch* trap rabbits (slang for "conning," as at
I.1.117)   32 *shift* employ fraud or trickery   35 *ken the wight* know the fellow (archaic and pretentious); *substance* holdings (i.e., he's rich)   38 *Two
yards* (Pistol jests at Falstaff's girth, playing on *what I am about* – i.e., "what
I'm planning" and "how big around I am")   41 *thrift* profit   42 *entertainment* (1) maintenance, financial support, (2) amusement, (3) receptiveness
43 *carves* i.e., (1) carves meat for her guests, (2) behaves suggestively; *the leer
of invitation* covert, flirtatious look   43–44 *construe* interpret (but more
specifically, translate; this speech and Pistol's response develop a series of linguistic metaphors – e.g., *Englished* – with Mrs. Ford as text and Falstaff as
reader)   44–45 *hardest voice* i.e., even the least favorable interpretation of
the most difficult passage

voice of her behavior, to be Englished rightly, is "I am
Sir John Falstaff's."

PISTOL   He hath studied her well, and translated her will,   47
out of honesty into English.   48

NYM   The anchor is deep. Will that humor pass?   49

FALSTAFF   Now, the report goes she has all the rule of her   50
husband's purse. He hath a legion of angels.   51

PISTOL   As many devils entertain – and "To her, boy,"
say I.

NYM   The humor rises – it is good. Humor me the angels.

FALSTAFF   I have writ me here a letter to her; and here an-   56
other to Page's wife, who even now gave me good eyes
too, examined my parts with most judicious oeillades.   58
Sometimes the beam of her view gilded my foot, some-   59
times my portly belly.   60

PISTOL   *[Aside]* Then did the sun on dunghill shine.

NYM   *[Aside]* I thank thee for that humor.

FALSTAFF   O, she did so course o'er my exteriors with
such a greedy intention that the appetite of her eye did
seem to scorch me up like a burning glass. Here's an-   65
other letter to her. She bears the purse too; she is a region in Guiana, all gold and bounty. I will be 'cheaters   67

---

47 *translated* (literally, "moved from one side to another"); *will* desires (probably with the specifically sexual sense of *will* as genitals – i.e., "he has read
her private parts")   48 *honesty* chastity, fidelity   49 *anchor . . . deep* i.e., the
plot is solid; *Will . . . pass* (1) How do you like the expression? (2) Will Falstaff's effort succeed?   51 *legion of angels* (a biblical joke: heavenly beings
were organized by *legion*, or "great number"; an *angel* is also an Elizabethan
coin stamped with an image of the archangel Michael – i.e., "Ford is rich")
56 *writ me* (like Nym's *Humor me* in the previous speech, an idiom that emphasizes the verb)   58 *parts* attractions; *oeillades* amorous glances (French)
59 *beam of her view* (according to Elizabethan physiology, vision resulted
from the eye's emitting beams that struck the object)   65 *burning glass* a
magnifying lens that starts a fire by concentrating the sun's rays   67 *Guiana*
(like *East and West Indies*, l. 69, a contemporary symbol of exotic wealth –
thanks in part to Sir Walter Ralegh's *Discovery of . . . Guiana,* published
1596, about his search for El Dorado); *'cheaters* (1) escheators, royal officers
in charge of property forfeited to the crown, (2) swindlers

68   to them both, and they shall be exchequers to me. They
      shall be my East and West Indies, and I will trade to
70   them both. Go, bear thou this letter to Mistress Page;
      and thou this to Mistress Ford. We will thrive, lads, we
      will thrive.

PISTOL
73   Shall I Sir Pandarus of Troy become,
74   And by my side wear steel? Then Lucifer take all!

NYM   I will run no base humor. Here, take the humor
76   letter. I will keep the havior of reputation.

FALSTAFF   *[To Robin]*
77   Hold, sirrah, bear you these letters titely:
78   Sail like my pinnace to these golden shores.

                                        [Exit Robin.]
79   Rogues, hence, avaunt! Vanish like hailstones, go;
80   Trudge, plod away o' the hoof; seek shelter, pack!
      Falstaff will learn the humor of the age:
82   French thrift, you rogues – myself and skirted page.

                                              [Exit.]
PISTOL
83   Let vultures gripe thy guts! for gourd and fullam holds,
84   And high and low beguiles the rich and poor.
85   Tester I'll have in pouch when thou shalt lack,
86   Base Phrygian Turk!

NYM   I have operations which be humors of revenge.

---

68 *exchequers* treasuries   **70–71** *Go . . . Ford* (neither F nor Q specifies who
is given which letter)   **73** *Sir Pandarus* the go-between in the medieval love
story of Troilus and Cressida, and thus the archetype of the bawd or pimp
74 *And . . . steel* i.e., and be both a warrior and a pimp   **76** *keep . . . reputation* i.e., maintain my good conduct and good name   **77** *titely* quickly   **78**
pinnace small, two-masted vessel, often accompanying a larger ship (as Robin
will do for Falstaff)   **79** *avaunt* away (an imperative dismissing evil spirits)
80 *pack* be off   **82** *French thrift* (an economy measure, to employ a single
servant instead of a retinue); *skirted* wearing the long four-paneled, skirted
coat of a servant   **83** *gripe* seize, grip; *gourd and fullam* (two names for false
dice); *holds* carries the day, is in fashion   **84** *high and low* i.e., dots on the
dice   **85** *Tester* (a coin; synecdoche for money in general)   **86** *Base Phrygian
Turk* (another of Pistol's pretentious, garbled insults; *Phrygia* = Troy)

PISTOL   Wilt thou revenge?

NYM   By welkin and her star!   89

PISTOL   With wit or steel?   90

NYM
With both the humors, I.
I will discuss the humor of this love to Page.   92

PISTOL
And I to Ford shall eke unfold   93
How Falstaff, varlet vile,   94
His dove will prove, his gold will hold,   95
And his soft couch defile.

NYM   My humor shall not cool. I will incense Page to
deal with poison. I will possess him with yellowness, for   98
the revolt of mine is dangerous. That is my true humor.   99

PISTOL   Thou art the Mars of malcontents. I second   100
thee; troop on.   *Exeunt.*

                              *

∿ **I.4** *Enter Mistress Quickly, Simple, [and] John Rugby.*

QUICKLY   What, John Rugby! I pray thee, go to the case-   1
ment and see if you can see my master, Master Doctor
Caius, coming. If he do, i' faith, and find anybody in
the house, here will be an old abusing of God's patience   4
and the King's English.

RUGBY   I'll go watch.

---

89 *welkin* heaven, sky   90 *wit or steel* i.e., scheme or violence   92 *discuss*
i.e., disclose   92–97 *to Page . . . to Ford . . . Page* (F has been emended to
make these speeches more nearly consistent with the action in II.1; it may be
that Shakespeare changed his mind about who informs which husband)   93
eke also   94 *varlet* (term of abuse)   95 *prove* test   98 *yellowness* (color associated with jealousy)   99 *the revolt . . . dangerous* i.e., my defection threatens
Falstaff (but *revolt* may mean "revulsion" or "disgust")   100 *Mars* i.e., god,
perfect image
    I.4 Inside Doctor Caius's house   1 *What* (expression of impatience:
"Hey!")   1–2 *casement* window   4 *an old* a plentiful, abundant

7 QUICKLY   Go, and we'll have a posset for't soon at night,
8   in faith, at the latter end of a sea-coal fire. *[Exit Rugby.]*
9   An honest, willing, kind fellow, as ever servant shall
10   come in house withal; and, I warrant you, no telltale,
11   nor no breedbate. His worst fault is, that he is given to
12   prayer; he is something peevish that way, but nobody
     but has his fault. But let that pass. – Peter Simple you
     say your name is?
     SIMPLE   Ay, for fault of a better.
     QUICKLY   And Master Slender's your master?
     SIMPLE   Ay, forsooth.
     QUICKLY   Does he not wear a great round beard like a
     glover's paring knife?
20   SIMPLE   No, forsooth. He hath but a little wee face, with
21   a little yellow beard – a Cain-colored beard.
22   QUICKLY   A softly sprighted man, is he not?
23   SIMPLE   Ay, forsooth. But he is as tall a man of his hands
24   as any is between this and his head: he hath fought with
25   a warrener.
     QUICKLY   How say you? O! I should remember him.
     Does he not hold up his head, as it were, and strut in
28   his gait?
     SIMPLE   Yes indeed does he.
30   QUICKLY   Well, heaven send Anne Page no worse for-
     tune. Tell Master Parson Evans I will do what I can for
     your master. Anne is a good girl, and I wish –
        [Enter Rugby.]
33   RUGBY   Out, alas, here comes my master!

---

7 *posset* hot drink of milk curdled with wine; *soon at night* as soon as night
comes   8 *sea-coal* (coal brought by sea from northern mines was superior to
ordinary charcoal: Caius is prosperous)   9–10 *as ever . . . withal* as any servant you'll find   11 *breedbate* troublemaker (*bate* = strife)   12 *peevish* foolish, or perhaps "headstrong, perverse"   20 *wee* tiny   21 *Cain-colored* i.e.,
reddish-yellow (the biblical murderer Cain was thus represented in religious
tapestries)   22 *softly sprighted* mild-spirited   23 *tall . . . hands* i.e., excellent
in action, valiant   24 *any . . . head* (proverbial expression meaning "around
here")   25 *warrener* gamekeeper   28 *gait* walk   33 *Out* (a mild oath or expression of concern: "Oh no!" "Dammit"; see also *Out upon't,* l. 154)

QUICKLY   We shall all be shent. Run in here, good young 34
man; go into this closet. He will not stay long. *[Pushes* 35
Simple into the next room.] What, John Rugby! John, 36
what, John, I say! Go, John, go inquire for my master. I
doubt he be not well, that he comes not home. 38
                              [Exit Rugby.]
[Sings.]
      "And down, down, adown-a," etc.
[Enter] Doctor [Caius].

CAIUS   Vat is you sing? I do not like des toys. Pray you go 40
and vetch me in my closset *une boîte en vert* – a box, a 41
green-a box. Do intend vat I speak? A green-a box. 42

QUICKLY   Ay, forsooth, I'll fetch it you. *[Aside]* I am glad
he went not in himself. If he had found the young man, 45
he would have been horn-mad.   *[Exit Quickly.]*

CAIUS   *Fe, fe, fe, fe! ma foi, il fait fort chaud. Je m'en vais à* 46
la cour – la grande affaire.
[Enter Quickly.]

QUICKLY   Is it this, sir?

CAIUS   *Oui; mette le au mon* pocket; *dépêche*, quickly. 49
Vere is dat knave Rugby? 50

QUICKLY   What, John Rugby? John!
[Enter Rugby.]

RUGBY   Here, sir.

CAIUS   You are John Rugby, and you are Jack Rugby. 53
Come, take-a your rapier and come after my heel to
the court.

---

34 *shent* disgraced   35 *closet* inner chamber, usually small (but not the modern storage room)   36–38 *What . . . home* (Quickly speaks loudly and ostentatiously, as if unaware of Caius's arrival)   38 *doubt* suspect, fear   40 *Vat* (the French doctor, like the Welsh parson, has trouble with English pronunciation; the comic deformations, which in the early texts are not consistent, are rough guides to the stage accent); *toys* trifles, frivolities   41 *une boîte en vert* a green box (but F's *vnboyteene* may be Shakespeare's French for "a little box")   42 *intend* hear (French *entendre*)   45 *horn-mad* fighting mad, like a horned animal and like a "horned" husband, a cuckold   46 *Fe* (an interjection of unknown origin)   46–47 *ma foi . . . affaire* by my faith, it is very hot; I am going to court – an important business   49 *Oui . . . pocket* yes, put it in my pocket   53 *Jack Rugby* (Caius's play on *jack* as [1] diminutive of *John,* [2] knave)

RUGBY   'Tis ready, sir, here in the porch.

57   CAIUS   By my trot, I tarry too long. – 'Od's me! *Qu'ai-*
58   *j'oublié?* Dere is some simples in my closset dat I vill
not for the varld I shall leave behind.

60   QUICKLY   *[Aside]* Ay me, he'll find the young man there,
and be mad.   *[Exit Caius.]*

62   CAIUS   *O diable! diable!* Vat is in my closset? Villainy!
63   *Larron! [Enter Caius, pulling Simple.]* Rugby, my rapier!

QUICKLY   Good master, be content.

CAIUS   Wherefore shall I be content-a?

QUICKLY   The young man is an honest man.

CAIUS   What shall de honest man do in my closset? Dere
is no honest man dat shall come in my closset.

69   QUICKLY   I beseech you, be not so phlegmatic. Hear the
70   truth of it: he came of an errand to me from Parson
Hugh.

CAIUS   Vell?

SIMPLE   Ay, forsooth, to desire her to –

QUICKLY   Peace, I pray you.

CAIUS   Peace-a your tongue. – Speak-a your tale.

SIMPLE   To desire this honest gentlewoman, your maid,
to speak a good word to Mistress Anne Page for my
master in the way of marriage.

79   QUICKLY   This is all, indeed, la; but I'll ne'er put my fin-
80   ger in the fire, and need not.

81   CAIUS   Sir Hugh send-a you? – Rugby, *baille* me some
paper. Tarry you a little-a while. *[Writes.]*

QUICKLY   *[Aside to Simple]* I am glad he is so quiet: if he
84   had been throughly moved, you should have heard him
85   so loud, and so melancholy. But notwithstanding, man,
I'll do you your master what good I can; and the very
yea and the no is, the French doctor, my master – I may

---

57 *trot* troth (truth); *'Od's me* God save me   57–58 *Qu'ai-j'oublié* what have
I forgotten   58 *simples* medicinal herbs (but with the obvious pun)   62 *diable* devil   63 *Larron* thief   69 *phlegmatic* (error for the "choleric" humor –
i.e., hot-tempered; *phlegmatic* = calm)   79–80 *put . . . not* i.e., I'll not meddle where it's not necessary (*and* = if)   81 *baille* fetch   84 *throughly* thoroughly, completely   85 *melancholy* surly, unpleasant

call him my master, look you, for I keep his house; and
I wash, wring, brew, bake, scour, dress meat and drink,   89
make the beds, and do all myself –   90

SIMPLE   *[Aside to Quickly]* 'Tis a great charge to come   91
under one body's hand.

QUICKLY   *[Aside to Simple]* Are you avised o' that? You
shall find it a great charge. And to be up early and
down late; but notwithstanding – to tell you in your   95
ear, I would have no words of it – my master himself is
in love with Mistress Anne Page. But notwithstanding
that, I know Anne's mind. That's neither here nor
there.

CAIUS   You jack'nape, give-a this letter to Sir Hugh. By   100
gar, it is a shallenge: I will cut his troat in de park; and
I will teach a scurvy jackanape priest to meddle or
make. You may be gone; it is not good you tarry here. –
By gar, I will cut all his two stones; by gar, he shall not   104
have a stone to throw at his dog.   *[Exit Simple.]*

QUICKLY   Alas, he speaks but for his friend.

CAIUS   It is no matter-a ver dat. Do not you tell-a me dat
I shall have Anne Page for myself? By gar, I vill kill de
jack priest; and I have appointed mine host of de Jar-   109
teer to measure our weapon. By gar, I will myself have   110
Anne Page.

QUICKLY   Sir, the maid loves you, and all shall be well.
We must give folks leave to prate – what the goodyear!   113

CAIUS   Rugby, come to the court with me. By gar, if I
have not Anne Page, I shall turn your head out of my
door. Follow my heels, Rugby.   *[Exeunt Caius
and Rugby.]*

---

89 *dress meat* prepare food   **91** *charge* responsibility   **95** *notwithstanding*
(Quickly's language, here as everywhere, is potentially bawdy: when she
complains about being overworked [*up early and down late*, ll. 94–95], the
undertone is that it is *not with standing* – i.e., not with sexual activity
[*standing* = erection])   **100** *jack'nape* jackanapes, ape (term of contempt)   **100–1** *By gar* (Caius's version of "by God")   **104** *stones* testicles
109 *jack* i.e., knavish   **110** *measure our weapon* make sure that they are equal
113 *prate* gossip; *what the goodyear* (expression of disgust or impatience)

117 QUICKLY   You shall have An – fool's head of your own. No, I know Anne's mind for that. Never a woman in Windsor knows more of Anne's mind than I do, nor
120   can do more than I do with her, I thank heaven.

FENTON   *[Within]* Who's within there, ho?

122 QUICKLY   Who's there, I trow? Come near the house, I pray you.
     [Enter] Fenton.

FENTON   How now, good woman, how dost thou?

QUICKLY   The better that it pleases your good worship to ask.

FENTON   What news? How does pretty Mistress Anne?

128 QUICKLY   In truth, sir, and she is pretty, and honest, and
129   gentle; and one that is your friend, I can tell you that by
130   the way, I praise heaven for it.

FENTON   Shall I do any good, think'st thou? Shall I not lose my suit?

QUICKLY   Troth, sir, all is in his hands above. But notwithstanding, Master Fenton, I'll be sworn on a book she loves you. Have not your worship a wart above your eye?

FENTON   Yes, marry have I. What of that?

138 QUICKLY   Well, thereby hangs a tale. Good faith, it is
139   such another Nan; but, I detest, an honest maid as ever
140   broke bread. We had an hour's talk of that wart. I shall never laugh but in that maid's company. But, indeed,
142   she is given too much to allicholy and musing. But for
143   you – well, go to.

FENTON   Well, I shall see her today. Hold, there's money for thee: let me have thy voice in my behalf. If thou seest her before me, commend me.

---

117 *An – fool's . . . own* (ironic reversal as Caius exits: he will have not "Anne" but "an" idiot's plaything instead)   122 *trow* wonder; *Come near* i.e., enter   128 *honest* chaste   129 *gentle* (1) agreeable, (2) well-born; *friend* supporter, favorably disposed toward you (not "sweetheart" in this case)   138–39 *it is . . . Nan* i.e., Anne is a really remarkable girl (*Nan* is a nickname)   139 *detest* (error for "protest" – i.e., swear)   142 *allicholy* melancholy   143 *go to* never mind, that's enough

QUICKLY   Will I? I' faith, that we will. And I will tell your
worship more of the wart the next time we have confi-   148
dence, and of other wooers.
FENTON   Well, farewell. I am in great haste now.   *150*
QUICKLY   Farewell to your worship. *[Exit Fenton.]* Truly,
an honest gentleman. But Anne loves him not, for I
know Anne's mind as well as another does. Out upon't,
what have I forgot?   *Exit.*

                            *

❧ **II.1** *Enter Mistress Page [with a letter].*

MRS. PAGE   What, have I scaped love letters in the holi-   1
day time of my beauty, and am I now a subject for
them? Let me see. *[Reads.]*
"Ask me no reason why I love you; for though Love use   4
Reason for his precisian, he admits him not for his
counselor. You are not young, no more am I. Go to
then, there's sympathy. You are merry, so am I. Ha, ha!   7
then there's more sympathy. You love sack, and so do I.   8
Would you desire better sympathy? Let it suffice thee,
Mistress Page – at the least, if the love of soldier can   *10*
suffice – that I love thee. I will not say, pity me – 'tis
not a soldierlike phrase – but I say, love me. By me,
                    Thine own true knight,
                    By day or night
                    Or any kind of light,
                    With all his might
                    For thee to fight,
                            John Falstaff."

148–49 *confidence* (error for "conference")
    II.1 Before the Pages' house   **1–2** *holiday* festive (i.e., youthful)   **4–6**
Love . . . counselor i.e., Love (personified) employs Reason as his official in-
structor (*precisian* = puritan, or strict master), but pays no real attention to
him   **7** *sympathy* affinity, similarity   **8** *sack* Spanish wine

19   What a Herod of Jewry is this! O wicked, wicked
20   world. One that is well-nigh worn to pieces with age, to
21   show himself a young gallant? What an unweighed be-
22   havior hath this Flemish drunkard picked – with the
23   devil's name! – out of my conversation that he dares in
      this manner assay me? Why, he hath not been thrice in
25   my company. What should I say to him? I was then fru-
26   gal of my mirth! Heaven forgive me! Why, I'll exhibit a
27   bill in the parliament for the putting down of men.
      How shall I be revenged on him? for revenged I will be,
29   as sure as his guts are made of puddings.
      [Enter] Mistress Ford.
30   MRS. FORD   Mistress Page! Trust me, I was going to your
      house.
      MRS. PAGE   And, trust me, I was coming to you. You look
      very ill.
34   MRS. FORD   Nay, I'll ne'er believe that. I have to show to
      the contrary.
      MRS. PAGE   Faith, but you do, in my mind.
      MRS. FORD   Well, I do then; yet I say I could show you to
      the contrary. O Mistress Page, give me some counsel.
      MRS. PAGE   What's the matter, woman?
40   MRS. FORD   O woman, if it were not for one trifling re-
41   spect, I could come to such honor.
      MRS. PAGE   Hang the trifle, woman; take the honor.
      What is it? Dispense with trifles; what is it?
44   MRS. FORD   If I would but go to hell for an eternal mo-
      ment or so, I could be knighted.

---

19 *Herod of Jewry* stage tyrant in medieval mystery plays, known for ranting,
pompous speech   21 *unweighed* ill-considered, thoughtless   22 *Flemish
drunkard* (residents of the Low Countries were famous for heavy drinking –
another stage stereotype)   23 *conversation* conduct (i.e., social interaction)
25 *What . . . say* i.e., what could I have possibly said   26 *exhibit* (formal
term for introducing a parliamentary *bill*)   27 *putting down* suppression,
disempowering   29 *puddings* sausages stuffed with meat, suet, and spices
34–35 *I have . . . contrary* i.e., I'm carrying proof that I look good   40–41
trifling respect i.e., trivial consideration   41 *honor* status, rank   44 *go to hell*
(the punishment for adultery)   44–45 *an eternal moment* a momentary indiscretion with everlasting consequences

MRS. PAGE What? thou liest. Sir Alice Ford? These
knights will hack; and so thou shouldst not alter the ar- 47
ticle of thy gentry.

MRS. FORD We burn daylight. Here, read, read: perceive 49
how I might be knighted. I shall think the worse of fat 50
men as long as I have an eye to make difference of
men's liking. And yet he would not swear; praised 52
women's modesty; and gave such orderly and well-
behaved reproof to all uncomeliness that I would have 54
sworn his disposition would have gone to the truth of 55
his words. But they do no more adhere and keep place
together than the Hundredth Psalm to the tune of 57
"Greensleeves." What tempest, I trow, threw this whale,
with so many tuns of oil in his belly, ashore at Wind- 59
sor? How shall I be revenged on him? I think the best 60
way were to entertain him with hope till the wicked fire 61
of lust have melted him in his own grease. Did you ever
hear the like?

MRS. PAGE Letter for letter, but that the name of Page
and Ford differs. To thy great comfort in this mystery 65
of ill opinions, here's the twin brother of thy letter. But
let thine inherit first, for I protest mine never shall. I 67
warrant he hath a thousand of these letters, writ with
blank space for different names – sure, more – and
these are of the second edition. He will print them, out 70
of doubt; for he cares not what he puts into the press, 71

---

47 *hack* i.e., play or fight with swords (a phallic metaphor: "hackney" is slang
for "whore")   47–48 *alter . . . gentry* change the terms (*article*) of your rank
49 *burn daylight* waste time   52 *liking* looks (i.e., what makes them likable)
54 *reproof . . . uncomeliness* disapproval of all improper conduct   55 *gone to*
matched   57–58 *Hundredth Psalm . . . "Greensleeves"* (the text of Psalm 100,
"Make a joyful noise unto the Lord," would clash with the music of the popular love song, just as Falstaff's meaning [*disposition*] conflicts with *the truth
of his words*)   59 *tuns* barrels   61 *entertain . . . hope* i.e., lead him on   65–66
mystery . . . opinions enigma concerning bad reputations   67 *inherit first* i.e.,
take precedence (primogeniture made the birth order of twins an important
legal matter)   70 *second edition* second printing (of another *thousand . . . letters*)   71 *into the press* (quibble on "printing press" and the "pressing down"
of women during sexual intercourse – a joke intensified by Falstaff's girth)

72   when he would put us two. I had rather be a giantess
and lie under Mount Pelion. Well, I will find you
74   twenty lascivious turtles ere one chaste man.

MRS. FORD   Why, this is the very same: the very hand,
the very words. What doth he think of us?

MRS. PAGE   Nay, I know not. It makes me almost ready
78   to wrangle with mine own honesty. I'll entertain myself
like one that I am not acquainted withal; for sure, un-
80   less he know some strain in me that I know not myself,
81   he would never have boarded me in this fury.

MRS. FORD   Boarding call you it? I'll be sure to keep him
above deck.

MRS. PAGE   So will I. If he come under my hatches, I'll
never to sea again. Let's be revenged on him. Let's appoint him a meeting, give him a show of comfort in his
87   suit, and lead him on with a fine-baited delay till he
hath pawned his horses to mine host of the Garter.

MRS. FORD   Nay, I will consent to act any villainy against
90   him that may not sully the chariness of our honesty. O
that my husband saw this letter! It would give eternal
food to his jealousy.

93   MRS. PAGE   Why, look where he comes, and my goodman too. He's as far from jealousy as I am from giving
him cause; and that, I hope, is an unmeasurable distance.

MRS. FORD   You are the happier woman.

MRS. PAGE   Let's consult together against this greasy
knight. Come hither. *[They talk privately.]*
[Enter] Master Page, [with] Nym, [and] Master Ford,
[with] Pistol.

72–73 *giantess . . . Pelion* (when giants challenged Zeus by piling Mount Pelion on Mount Ossa to reach Olympus, he imprisoned them beneath the
mountains)   74 *lascivious turtles* promiscuous turtledoves (an oxymoron:
turtledoves were famously constant)   78 *wrangle . . . honesty* i.e., doubt or
dispute my own chastity; *entertain myself* behave   80 *strain* feature, quality
81 *boarded me* attacked me (a naval metaphor of aggression or piracy)   87 *a
fine-baited* an alluring (like an irresistible fishing lure)   90 *sully . . . honesty*
i.e., stain our carefully guarded chastity   93–94 *goodman* husband

FORD   Well, I hope it be not so.   100

PISTOL

Hope is a curtal dog in some affairs.   101

Sir John affects thy wife.   102

FORD   Why, sir, my wife is not young.

PISTOL

He woos both high and low, both rich and poor,

Both young and old, one with another, Ford.

He loves the gallimaufry. Ford, perpend.   106

FORD   Love my wife?

PISTOL

With liver burning hot. Prevent, or go thou,   108

Like Sir Actaeon he, with Ringwood at thy heels. –

O, odious is the name!   *110*

FORD   What name, sir?

PISTOL

The horn, I say. Farewell.

Take heed, have open eye, for thieves do foot by night.

Take heed, ere summer comes or cuckoo birds do sing.   114

Away, Sir Corporal Nym!

Believe it, Page; he speaks sense.   *[Exit.]*

FORD   *[Aside]* I will be patient; I will find out this.

NYM   *[To Page]* And this is true; I like not the humor of
lying. He hath wronged me in some humors. I should
have borne the humored letter to her, but I have a   120
sword and it shall bite upon my necessity. He loves
your wife – there's the short and the long. My name is

---

101 *curtal dog* tail-docked dog (i.e., *Hope* is diminished or damaged [?])
102 *affects* is attracted to, loves   106 *gallimaufry* stew made from a number
of ingredients; *perpend* pay attention   108 *liver* (thought to be the seat of
passionate love)   108–9 *go thou . . . Ringwood* (Pistol threatens Ford with
the cuckold's horns by alluding to the myth of *Actaeon*, whose punishment
for watching Diana at her bath was to be turned into a horned stag and torn
apart by his hunting dogs); *Ringwood* (the name of one of those dogs in
Golding's 1567 translation of the myth from Ovid's *Metamorphoses*)   114
cuckoo birds (with a call that sounds like "cuckold" and a habit of laying its
eggs in other birds' nests, the cuckoo reminds the betrayed husband of his
shame)   120 *humored letter* (another vague use of Nym's favorite word
"humor" – perhaps meaning something like the modern "damn letter")

Corporal Nym; I speak, and I avouch 'tis true. My
name is Nym, and Falstaff loves your wife. Adieu. I love
125   not the humor of bread and cheese, and there's the
humor of it. Adieu.   *[Exit.]*
127   PAGE   "The humor of it," quoth a! Here's a fellow frights
128   English out of his wits.
FORD   *[Aside]* I will seek out Falstaff.
130   PAGE   *[Aside]* I never heard such a drawling, affecting
rogue.
FORD   *[Aside]* If I do find it – well.
133   PAGE   *[Aside]* I will not believe such a Cataian, though
the priest o' the town commended him for a true man.
FORD   *[Aside]* 'Twas a good sensible fellow – well.
[Mistress Page and Mistress Ford come forward.]
PAGE   How now, Meg?
MRS. PAGE   Whither go you, George? Hark you.
[Whispers.]
MRS. FORD   How now, sweet Frank? Why art thou
melancholy?
140   FORD   I melancholy? I am not melancholy. Get you
home, go.
142   MRS. FORD   Faith, thou hast some crotchets in thy head
now. Will you go, Mistress Page?
MRS. PAGE   Have with you. – You'll come to dinner,
George? *[Aside to Mistress Ford]* Look who comes yon-
der. She shall be our messenger to this paltry knight.
[Enter] Mistress Quickly.
MRS. FORD   *[Aside to Mistress Page]* Trust me, I thought
148   on her: she'll fit it.
MRS. PAGE   You are come to see my daughter Anne?
150   QUICKLY   Ay, forsooth; and I pray, how does good Mistress Anne?

---

125 *bread and cheese* i.e., mere necessities (Nym presents himself as re-
spectable, better than a beggar)   127 *a* he   128 *his* its   130 *drawling* slow-
speaking; *affecting* pretentious, affected   133 *Cataian* scoundrel (from
"Cathayan," Chinese man)   142 *crotchets* fancies, wild ideas   148 *fit it* fill
the need

MRS. PAGE   Go in with us and see. We have an hour's talk
with you.   *[Exeunt Mistress Page, Mistress Ford,
and Mistress Quickly.]*

PAGE   How now, Master Ford?

FORD   You heard what this knave told me, did you not?

PAGE   Yes, and you heard what the other told me?

FORD   Do you think there is truth in them?

PAGE   Hang 'em, slaves! I do not think the knight would
offer it. But these that accuse him in his intent towards   159
our wives are a yoke of his discarded men – very rogues,   160
now they be out of service.

FORD   Were they his men?

PAGE   Marry were they.

FORD   I like it never the better for that. Does he lie at the
Garter?

PAGE   Ay, marry does he. If he should intend this voyage
toward my wife, I would turn her loose to him; and
what he gets more of her than sharp words, let it lie on   168
my head.

FORD   I do not misdoubt my wife, but I would be loath   170
to turn them together. A man may be too confident. I   171
would have nothing lie on my head. I cannot be thus
satisfied.

PAGE   Look where my ranting host of the Garter comes.
      [Enter] Host.
There is either liquor in his pate or money in his purse   175
when he looks so merrily. How now, mine host?

HOST   How now, bullyrook? Thou'rt a gentleman. Cav-   177
aliero Justice, I say!
      [Enter] Shallow.

---

159 *offer* attempt, dare   160 *yoke* pair   168–69 *lie on my head* be charged to
me (with pun on the cuckold's unseen horns)   171 *turn them together* pas-
ture them together (with the likelihood of copulation – a metaphor from animal husbandry)   175 *pate* head (i.e., he's drunk)   177–78 *Cavaliero Justice*
i.e., "Gallant Judge"

179   SHALLOW   I follow, mine host, I follow. Good even and
180   twenty, good Master Page. Master Page, will you go
    with us? We have sport in hand.

    HOST   Tell him, Cavaliero Justice; tell him, bullyrook.

    SHALLOW   Sir, there is a fray to be fought between Sir
    Hugh the Welsh priest and Caius the French doctor.

    FORD   Good mine host o' the Garter, a word with you.

    HOST   What sayst thou, my bullyrook?

    [They go aside.]

    SHALLOW   *[To Page]* Will you go with us to behold it?
    My merry host hath had the measuring of their
189   weapons, and, I think, hath appointed them contrary
190   places; for, believe me, I hear the parson is no jester.
    Hark, I will tell you what our sport shall be.

    [They go aside.]

192   HOST   Hast thou no suit against my knight, my Guest
    Cavaliero?

194   FORD   None, I protest. But I'll give you a pottle of
195   burned sack to give me recourse to him and tell him my
    name is Brook — only for a jest.

    HOST   My hand, bully. Thou shalt have egress and
    regress — said I well? — and thy name shall be Brook. It
199   is a merry knight. Will you go, *asniers?*

200   SHALLOW   Have with you, mine host.

    PAGE   I have heard the Frenchman hath good skill in his
    rapier.

    SHALLOW   Tut, sir, I could have told you more. In these
204   times you stand on distance, your passes, stoccadoes,
    and I know not what. 'Tis the heart, Master Page; 'tis

179–80 *Good . . . twenty* good evening and twenty more of them (an error, either the Host's or Shakespeare's, since it is still morning in play time)   **189** *contrary* opposing   **192–93** *my knight . . . Cavaliero* i.e., Falstaff, a guest at the Garter Inn   **194** *protest* insist, declare; *pottle* large tankard   **195** *burned sack* warmed Spanish wine   **195** *recourse* access   **199** *asniers* mule drivers (French; some editors print "mynheers" [Dutch], sirs – i.e., "my masters"; F reads "An-heires")   **204** *stand on . . . stoccadoes* (description of tactics on which swordsmen depend, stand on); *distance* space between fencers; *passes* lunges; *stoccadoes* thrusts (Shallow deplores the modern concentration on technique, as opposed to the *heart*, l. 205 – i.e., courage – demanded in his day)

here, 'tis here. I have seen the time with my long sword
I would have made you four tall fellows skip like rats.

HOST   Here, boys, here, here! Shall we wag?

PAGE   Have with you. I had rather hear them scold than
fight.   *[Exeunt Host, Shallow, and Page.]*   210

FORD   Though Page be a secure fool and stands so firmly   211
on his wife's frailty, yet I cannot put off my opinion so
easily. She was in his company at Page's house, and
what they made there, I know not. Well, I will look fur-   214
ther into't; and I have a disguise to sound Falstaff. If I   215
find her honest, I lose not my labor. If she be otherwise,
'tis labor well bestowed.   *[Exit.]*

*

◦ **II.2** *Enter Falstaff, [and] Pistol.*

FALSTAFF   I will not lend thee a penny.

PISTOL
Why, then the world's mine oyster,
Which I with sword will open.

FALSTAFF   Not a penny. I have been content, sir, you
should lay my countenance to pawn. I have grated   5
upon my good friends for three reprieves for you and
your coachfellow Nym, or else you had looked through   7
the grate, like a geminy of baboons. I am damned in   8
hell for swearing to gentlemen my friends, you were
good soldiers and tall fellows; and when Mistress Brid-   10
get lost the handle of her fan, I took't upon mine honor   11
thou hadst it not.

---

211 *a secure* an overconfident   211–12 *stands . . . frailty* i.e., foolishly puts
his faith in a weak female   214 *made* did, performed   215 *sound* test, measure the depth of
    II.2 A room in the Garter Inn   5 *lay my . . . pawn* borrow money on the
strength of my standing (*countenance*)   5–6 *grated upon* irritated   7 *coachfellow* companion (as if they were a team of horses)   8 *grate* i.e., barred
prison window; *geminy of baboons* twin ("Gemini") apes   10 *tall* valiant   11
took't took an oath

PISTOL
>   Didst thou not share? Hadst thou not fifteen pence?

FALSTAFF   Reason, you rogue, reason: think'st thou, I'll
15   endanger my soul gratis? At a word, hang no more
16   about me: I am no gibbet for you. Go! a short knife and
17   a throng! – to your manor of Pickt-hatch, go. You'll
>   not bear a letter for me, you rogue? You stand upon
>   your honor! Why, thou unconfinable baseness, it is as
20   much as I can do to keep the terms of my honor
>   precise. I, ay, I myself sometimes, leaving the fear of
22   God on the left hand and hiding mine honor in my
23   necessity, am fain to shuffle, to hedge, and to lurch;
24   and yet you, rogue, will ensconce your rags, your cat-
>   a-mountain looks, your red-lattice phrases, and your
>   bold-beating oaths, under the shelter of your honor!
>   You will not do it, you!

PISTOL
>   I do relent. What would thou more of man?
>   *[Enter] Robin.*

ROBIN   Sir, here's a woman would speak with you.
30   FALSTAFF   Let her approach.
>   *[Enter Mistress] Quickly.*

QUICKLY   Give your worship good morrow.
32   FALSTAFF   Good morrow, goodwife.
33   QUICKLY   Not so, and't please your worship.
>   FALSTAFF   Good maid then.

---

15 *gratis* for nothing   16 *gibbet* gallows (pun following from *hang no more
about me*, ll. 15–16)   16–17 *short . . . throng* i.e., all you need is a short knife
to cut purse strings in a crowd of people   17 *manor of Pickt-hatch* (probably
a brothel in a disreputable section of London – i.e., the opposite of a manor
house)   20–21 *the terms . . . precise* i.e., my reputation pure   22 *on the left
hand* i.e., to one side, so I won't think about it   23 *fain . . . lurch* i.e., forced
to swindle and deceive: *lurch* = (1) lurk or hide, (2) steal   24–26 *ensconce . . . honor* i.e., use your "honor" to conceal your filthy, wild (*cat-a-
mountain*) appearance, tavern speech, and bluster (*oaths*)   32 *goodwife*
("wife" was the general term for a married woman, as opposed to *maid*
[l. 34], the general term for an unmarried woman)   33 *and't* if it ("and" or
"an" can mean "if")

QUICKLY I'll be sworn, as my mother was, the first hour 35
I was born.
FALSTAFF I do believe the swearer. What with me?
QUICKLY Shall I vouchsafe your worship a word or two? 38
FALSTAFF Two thousand, fair woman, and I'll vouchsafe
thee the hearing.   40
QUICKLY There is one Mistress Ford, sir – I pray, come a
little nearer this ways. I myself dwell with Master Doc-   42
tor Caius.
FALSTAFF Well, on; Mistress Ford, you say –   44
QUICKLY Your worship says very true – I pray your wor-
ship, come a little nearer this ways.
FALSTAFF I warrant thee nobody hears – mine own
people, mine own people.
QUICKLY Are they so? God bless them and make them
his servants! *[They go aside.]*   50
FALSTAFF Well, Mistress Ford – what of her?
QUICKLY Why, sir, she's a good creature. Lord, Lord,
your worship's a wanton! Well, God forgive you, and all   53
of us, I pray.
FALSTAFF Mistress Ford – come, Mistress Ford –
QUICKLY Marry, this is the short and the long of it. You
have brought her into such a canaries as 'tis wonderful.   57
The best courtier of them all, when the court lay at
Windsor, could never have brought her to such a canary. Yet there has been knights, and lords, and gen-   60
tlemen, with their coaches. I warrant you, coach after
coach, letter after letter, gift after gift; smelling so
sweetly – all musk – and so rushling, I warrant you, in   63
silk and gold; and in such alligant terms; and in such   64

35–36 *as . . . born* i.e., not a virgin (*maid*) **38** *vouchsafe* grant **42, 46** *this ways* (variation on "this way" – i.e., toward me: Quickly is concerned, as Falstaff's reply in ll. 47–48 makes clear, about speaking in the presence of Pistol and Robin) **44** *on* go on **53** *wanton* rogue **57** *canaries* state of anxiety (Quickly probably means "quandary") **63** *rushling* (error for "rustling") **64** *alligant* (either "elegant" or "eloquent," and perhaps suggesting "alicante," a Spanish wine, since *wine and sugar* as gifts immediately follow)

wine and sugar of the best and the fairest that would
have won any woman's heart; and I warrant you they
could never get an eyewink of her. I had myself twenty
68 angels given me this morning; but I defy all angels – in
any such sort, as they say – but in the way of honesty;
70 and I warrant you they could never get her so much as
sip on a cup with the proudest of them all; and yet
72 there has been earls – nay, which is more, pensioners;
73 but, I warrant you, all is one with her.

FALSTAFF   But what says she to me? Be brief, my good
75 she-Mercury.

QUICKLY   Marry, she hath received your letter; for the
which she thanks you a thousand times; and she gives
you to notify that her husband will be absence from his
house between ten and eleven.

80 FALSTAFF   Ten and eleven.

81 QUICKLY   Ay, forsooth; and then you may come and see
82 the picture, she says, that you wot of. Master Ford her
husband will be from home. Alas, the sweet woman
leads an ill life with him; he's a very jealousy man; she
85 leads a very frampold life with him, good heart.

FALSTAFF   Ten and eleven. Woman, commend me to her;
I will not fail her.

QUICKLY   Why, you say well. But I have another messenger to your worship. Mistress Page hath her hearty
90 commendations to you too; and let me tell you in your
91 ear, she's as fartuous a civil modest wife, and one, I tell
92 you, that will not miss you morning nor evening
93 prayer, as any is in Windsor, whoe'er be the other; and

68–69 *defy ... honesty* reject money (*angels* = coins) offered for improper
business (with a joke on *defy all angels* – i.e., challenge all the heavenly hosts)
72 *pensioners* gentlemen bodyguards of the sovereign (or perhaps poor
knights of Windsor – i.e., retired servicemen supported by royal charity)
73 *all is one ... her* she responds similarly (i.e., negatively) to all   75 *she-
Mercury* messenger (as Mercury served Zeus)   81–82 *see the picture* (pretext
for a shady meeting)   82 *wot* know   85 *frampold* quarrelsome, unpleasant
91 *fartuous* (error for "virtuous")   92 *miss you* (as in *writ me*, I.3.56, the pronoun merely emphasizes the verb)   93 *whoe'er ... other* i.e., put any woman
up against her

she bade me tell your worship that her husband is sel-
dom from home, but she hopes there will come a time.
I never knew a woman so dote upon a man. Surely I
think you have charms, la; yes, in truth.   97

FALSTAFF   Not I, I assure thee. Setting the attraction of
my good parts aside, I have no other charms.   99

QUICKLY   Blessing on your heart for't!   *100*

FALSTAFF   But, I pray thee, tell me this: has Ford's wife
and Page's wife acquainted each other how they love
me?

QUICKLY   That were a jest indeed! They have not so little
grace, I hope; that were a trick indeed! But Mistress   105
Page would desire you to send her your little page, of all   106
loves; her husband has a marvelous infection to the lit-   107
tle page; and truly Master Page is an honest man. Never
a wife in Windsor leads a better life than she does. Do
what she will, say what she will, take all, pay all, go to   *110*
bed when she list, rise when she list, all is as she will.   111
And truly she deserves it; for if there be a kind woman
in Windsor, she is one. You must send her your page –
no remedy.

FALSTAFF   Why, I will.

QUICKLY   Nay, but do so then; and look you, he may
come and go between you both; and in any case have a
nayword, that you may know one another's mind, and   118
the boy never need to understand anything; for 'tis not
good that children should know any wickedness. Old   *120*
folks, you know, have discretion, as they say, and know
the world.

FALSTAFF   Fare thee well, commend me to them both.
There's my purse; I am yet thy debtor. Boy, go along   124

---

97 *charms* magic spells, powers of enchantment   99 *parts* talents, attractions
(not merely physical, but Falstaff may emphasize the vulgar sense of *parts*)
105 *grace* sense of what is proper   106–7 *of all loves* for the sake of love
107 *infection* (error for "affection")   111 *list* likes   118 *nayword* password,
signal   124 *yet* still (Falstaff acknowledges his payment – *There's my purse* –
as inadequate)

with this woman. *[Exeunt Mistress Quickly and Robin.]*
This news distracts me.

PISTOL   *[Aside]*
127   This punk is one of Cupid's carriers.
128   Clap on more sails, pursue, up with your fights!
129   Give fire! She is my prize, or ocean whelm them all!

[Exit.]

130   FALSTAFF   Sayst thou so, old Jack? Go thy ways; I'll
make more of thy old body than I have done. Will they
yet look after thee? Wilt thou, after the expense of so
much money, be now a gainer? Good body, I thank
134   thee. Let them say 'tis grossly done; so it be fairly done,
no matter.
[Enter] Bardolph.

136   BARDOLPH   Sir John, there's one Master Brook below
would fain speak with you, and be acquainted with
138   you; and hath sent your worship a morning's draught
of sack.

140   FALSTAFF   Brook is his name?

BARDOLPH   Ay, sir.

FALSTAFF   Call him in. *[Exit Bardolph.]* Such Brooks are
welcome to me, that o'erflows such liquor. Ah ha! Mis-
144   tress Ford and Mistress Page, have I encompassed you?
145   Go to; via!
[Enter Bardolph, with] Ford [disguised].

146   FORD   'Bless you, sir.

FALSTAFF   And you, sir; would you speak with me?

***

127 *punk* prostitute; *carriers* messengers, agents **128** *fights* protective
screens used on deck in sea battles **129** *Give fire* shoot the cannon; *prize*
captured ship; *ocean whelm* i.e., let the ocean submerge (Pistol's outburst
may be related to *Henry V,* in which he is married to Mistress Quickly) **134**
grossly badly, sloppily (but with play on *gross* as "obese") **136** *Master Brook*
(F reads "Broome" throughout; the original "Brooke" of Q was probably altered because it offended the powerful Lord Cobham, whose family name
was Brooke; see Note on the Text, page xliii–xliv) **138–39** *draught of sack*
drink of wine **144** *encompassed* got possession of **145** *via* (shout of encouragement, Italian) **146** *'Bless you* (the apostrophe implies the dropping
of "God" in "God bless you"; on censorship, see Note on the Text, p. liii)

FORD   I make bold to press with so little preparation   148
upon you.

FALSTAFF   You're welcome. What's your will? – Give us   150
leave, drawer.   *[Exit Bardolph.]*

FORD   Sir, I am a gentleman that have spent much. My
name is Brook.

FALSTAFF   Good Master Brook, I desire more acquaintance of you.

FORD   Good Sir John, I sue for yours – not to charge   156
you – for I must let you understand I think myself in
better plight for a lender than you are, the which hath
something emboldened me to this unseasoned intru-   159
sion; for they say if money go before, all ways do lie   160
open.

FALSTAFF   Money is a good soldier, sir, and will on.

FORD   Troth, and I have a bag of money here troubles
me. If you will help to bear it, Sir John, take all, or half,
for easing me of the carriage.   165

FALSTAFF   Sir, I know not how I may deserve to be your
porter.

FORD   I will tell you, sir, if you will give me the hearing.

FALSTAFF   Speak, good Master Brook. I shall be glad to
be your servant.   170

FORD   Sir, I hear you are a scholar – I will be brief with
you – and you have been a man long known to me,
though I had never so good means as desire to make   173
myself acquainted with you. I shall discover a thing to   174
you wherein I must very much lay open mine own im-
perfection; but, good Sir John, as you have one eye
upon my follies, as you hear them unfolded, turn another into the register of your own, that I may pass   178

---

148 *preparation* warning, notice   150–51 *Give . . . drawer* (Falstaff dismisses Bardolph the bartender)   156 *sue for* request; *charge* be an expense to
159 *unseasoned* ill-timed, unseasonable   165 *easing* relieving; *carriage* bur-
den of carrying it   173 *never . . . desire* i.e., my opportunity (*means*) for
meeting you was always less than my wish   174 *discover* reveal, disclose
178 *register* list, record   178–79 *pass . . . easier* i.e., get by with milder disapproval

179 with a reproof the easier, sith you yourself know how
180 easy it is to be such an offender.

FALSTAFF Very well, sir; proceed.

FORD There is a gentlewoman in this town, her husband's name is Ford.

FALSTAFF Well, sir.

FORD I have long loved her, and, I protest to you, bestowed much on her, followed her with a doting obser-
187 vance, engrossed opportunities to meet her, feed every
188 slight occasion that could but niggardly give me sight
of her, not only bought many presents to give her but
190 have given largely to many to know what she would
have given. Briefly, I have pursued her as love hath pursued me, which hath been on the wing of all occasions.
But whatsoever I have merited – either in my mind or
194 in my means – meed, I am sure, I have received none,
unless experience be a jewel. That I have purchased at
an infinite rate, and that hath taught me to say this,
197 "Love like a shadow flies when substance love
       pursues;
Pursuing that that flies, and flying what pursues."

FALSTAFF Have you received no promise of satisfaction
200 at her hands?

FORD Never.

202 FALSTAFF Have you importuned her to such a purpose?

FORD Never.

204 FALSTAFF Of what quality was your love then?

FORD Like a fair house built on another man's ground,
so that I have lost my edifice by mistaking the place
207 where I erected it.

---

179 *sith* since   187 *engrossed* collected   187–88 *feed . . . occasion* taken advantage of every opportunity (*feed* = hired)   188 *but niggardly* even slightly
190–91 *would have given* prefers to receive   194 *in my means* i.e., by virtue
of my outlay; *meed* reward   197–98 *Love . . . what pursues* (a verse adaptation of the proverb "Love, like a shadow, flies one following and pursues one
fleeing"; there is also a play on *substance* as [1] opposite of *shadow,* [2] wealth)
202 *importuned* approached, begged   204 *quality* kind   207 *erected* (perhaps with a sexual undertone)

FALSTAFF To what purpose have you unfolded this to 208
me?

FORD When I have told you that, I have told you all. 210
Some say that though she appear honest to me, yet in 211
other places she enlargeth her mirth so far that there is 212
shrewd construction made of her. Now, Sir John, here 213
is the heart of my purpose: you are a gentleman of excellent breeding, admirable discourse, of great admit- 215
tance, authentic in your place and person, generally 216
allowed for your many warlike, courtlike, and learned 217
preparations.

FALSTAFF O sir!

FORD Believe it, for you know it. There is money. Spend 220
it, spend it; spend more; spend all I have. Only give me
so much of your time in exchange of it as to lay an ami- 222
able siege to the honesty of this Ford's wife. Use your
art of wooing, win her to consent to you; if any man
may, you may as soon as any.

FALSTAFF Would it apply well to the vehemency of your 226
affection that I should win what you would enjoy? Methinks you prescribe to yourself very preposterously.

FORD O, understand my drift. She dwells so securely on
the excellency of her honor that the folly of my soul 230
dares not present itself. She is too bright to be looked
against. Now, could I come to her with any detection 232
in my hand, my desires had instance and argument to 233
commend themselves. I could drive her then from the
ward of her purity, her reputation, her marriage vow, 235
and a thousand other her defenses, which now are

---

208 *unfolded* opened, revealed 211 *appear honest* pretends to chastity 212
enlargeth gives free rein to 213 *shrewd construction made* ugly inferences
drawn 215–16 *of great admittance* i.e., welcome in the highest social circles
216 *authentic* authoritative, respected 217 *allowed* approved 217–18
learned preparations scholarly attainments 222–23 *amiable* i.e., amorous
226 *apply well to* suit, be consistent with; *vehemency* passionate strength 230
folly i.e., uncontrollable feelings, lust 232 *against* directly at (like the sun);
detection evidence (i.e., knowledge of her misconduct) 233 *had . . . and argument* would have proof and a good case 235 *ward* defense, safety (a fencing term)

237   too too strongly embattled against me. What say you
       to't, Sir John?
239 FALSTAFF Master Brook, I will first make bold with your
240   money; next, give me your hand; and last, as I am a
       gentleman, you shall, if you will, enjoy Ford's wife.
     FORD O good sir!
     FALSTAFF I say you shall.
244 FORD Want no money, Sir John; you shall want none.
     FALSTAFF Want no Mistress Ford, Master Brook; you
       shall want none. I shall be with her, I may tell you, by
       her own appointment: even as you came in to me, her
       assistant or go-between parted from me. I say I shall be
       with her between ten and eleven, for at that time the
250   jealous rascally knave her husband will be forth. Come
251   you to me at night; you shall know how I speed.
     FORD I am blessed in your acquaintance. Do you know
       Ford, sir?
     FALSTAFF Hang him, poor cuckoldy knave! I know him
       not. Yet I wrong him to call him poor: they say the jeal-
256   ous wittolly knave hath masses of money; for the which
257   his wife seems to me well-favored. I will use her as the
258   key of the cuckoldy rogue's coffer, and there's my har-
       vest home.
260 FORD I would you knew Ford, sir, that you might avoid
       him if you saw him.
262 FALSTAFF Hang him, mechanical salt-butter rogue! I will
       stare him out of his wits. I will awe him with my cud-
       gel; it shall hang like a meteor o'er the cuckold's horns.
265   Master Brook, thou shalt know I will predominate over
266   the peasant, and thou shalt lie with his wife. Come to

---

237 *embattled* fortified   239 *make bold with* i.e., take, if you please   244
Want lack   250 *forth* i.e., out, away from home   251 *speed* get along (i.e.,
succeed)   256 *wittolly* (equivalent here of *cuckoldy,* l. 254; technically, a *wittol* is a husband who knows of and accepts his wife's adultery)   257 *well-favored* good-looking   258–59 *harvest home* i.e., final harvest (of my profit)
262 *mechanical salt-butter* (two class-based insults: *mechanical* = laboring;
salt-butter = cheap, imported butter, not fresh)   265 *predominate* gain ascen-
dancy (like a planet, according to astrology)   266 *peasant* rascal

me soon at night. Ford's a knave, and I will aggravate 267
his style. Thou, Master Brook, shalt know him for
knave and cuckold. Come to me soon at night. *[Exit.]*
FORD   What a damned Epicurean rascal is this! My heart 270
is ready to crack with impatience. Who says this is im- 271
provident jealousy? My wife hath sent to him, the hour
is fixed, the match is made. Would any man have
thought this? See the hell of having a false woman!
My bed shall be abused, my coffers ransacked, my reputation gnawn at; and I shall not only receive this
villainous wrong, but stand under the adoption of 277
abominable terms, and by him that does me this
wrong. Terms! names! Amaimon sounds well; Lucifer, 279
well; Barbason, well; yet they are devils' additions, the 280
names of fiends. But Cuckold! Wittol! Cuckold! The 281
devil himself hath not such a name. Page is an ass, a se- 282
cure ass. He will trust his wife; he will not be jealous.
I will rather trust a Fleming with my butter, Parson 284
Hugh the Welshman with my cheese, an Irishman with
my aqua vitae bottle, or a thief to walk my ambling 286
gelding, than my wife with herself. Then she plots,
then she ruminates, then she devises – and what they
think in their hearts they may effect, they will break
their hearts but they will effect. God be praised for my 290
jealousy. Eleven o'clock the hour. I will prevent this, de- 291
tect my wife, be revenged on Falstaff, and laugh at
Page. I will about it; better three hours too soon than a
minute too late. Fie, fie, fie! cuckold! cuckold! cuckold! 294
Exit.

*

267–68 *aggravate his style* i.e., add to his (shameful) title   270 *Epicurean*
sensual, pleasure-seeking   271–72 *improvident* hasty, unjustified   277–78
stand . . . terms be subject to name-calling   279–80 *Amaimon, Lucifer, Bar-*
bason (names of devils)   280 *additions* titles   281 *Wittol* (see l. 256 n.)
282–83 *a secure* an overconfident   284–85 *Fleming, Welshman, Irishman*
(accepted stereotypes: residents of the Low Countries loved butter, the Welsh
cheese, and the Irish liquor – *aqua vitae*)   286–87 *ambling gelding* gentle
riding horse   291 *prevent* intercept (literally "come before")   294 *Fie*
(strong expression of disgust)

∾ **II.3** *Enter [Doctor] Caius, [and] Rugby.*

CAIUS   Jack Rugby.

RUGBY   Sir?

CAIUS   Vat is the clock, Jack?

RUGBY   'Tis past the hour, sir, that Sir Hugh promised to
meet.

CAIUS   By gar, he has save his soul dat he is no come. He
has pray his Pible well dat he is no come. By gar, Jack
Rugby, he is dead already if he be come.

RUGBY   He is wise, sir. He knew your worship would kill
10   him if he came.

11 CAIUS   By gar, de herring is no dead so as I vill kill him.
Take your rapier, Jack; I vill tell you how I vill kill him.

RUGBY   Alas, sir, I cannot fence.

CAIUS   Villainy, take your rapier.

15 RUGBY   Forbear; here's company.
    [Enter] Page, Shallow, Slender, [and] Host.

HOST   God bless thee, bully doctor.

SHALLOW   God save you, Master Doctor Caius.

PAGE   Now, good Master Doctor.

19 SLENDER   'Give you good morrow, sir.

20 CAIUS   Vat be all you, one, two, tree, four, come for?

21 HOST   To see thee fight, to see thee foin, to see thee tra-
22   verse; to see thee here, to see thee there; to see thee pass
23   thy punto, thy stock, thy reverse, thy distance, thy
24   montant. Is he dead, my Ethiopian? Is he dead, my
25   Francisco? Ha, bully? What says my Aesculapius? my

II.3 A field near Windsor **11** *herring* (alluding to the proverbial "dead as a
herring") **15** *Forbear* i.e., restrain yourself **19** *'Give you* God give you **21**
foin thrust **21–22** *traverse* move from side to side (fencing terms) **22** *pass*
use, perform **23** *punto* thrust with the sword's point; *stock* stoccado
(thrust); *reverse* backhanded stroke; *distance* skillful separation from the opponent **24** *montant* upward thrust; *Ethiopian* i.e., swarthy man (the first of
the Host's blizzard of insults, which Caius doesn't understand) **25** *Francisco*
(the Host's coinage for "Frenchman"; cf. modern derogatory "Frenchy"); *Aesculapius* god of medicine

Galen? my heart of elder? Ha, is he dead, bully stale? is 26
he dead?

CAIUS   By gar, he is de coward jack priest of de vorld. He
is not show his face.

HOST   Thou art a Castalion King Urinal! Hector of 30
Greece, my boy!

CAIUS   I pray you bear witness that me have stay six or
seven, two, tree hours for him, and he is no come.

SHALLOW   He is the wiser man, Master Doctor. He is a
curer of souls, and you a curer of bodies. If you should
fight, you go against the hair of your professions. Is it 36
not true, Master Page?

PAGE   Master Shallow, you have yourself been a great
fighter, though now a man of peace.   39

SHALLOW   Bodykins, Master Page, though I now be old 40
and of the peace, if I see a sword out, my finger itches
to make one. Though we are justices and doctors and 42
churchmen, Master Page, we have some salt of our 43
youth in us. We are the sons of women, Master Page.

PAGE   'Tis true, Master Shallow.

SHALLOW   It will be found so, Master Page. Master Doctor Caius, I am come to fetch you home. I am sworn of
the peace. You have showed yourself a wise physician,
and Sir Hugh hath shown himself a wise and patient
churchman. You must go with me, Master Doctor.   50

---

26 *Galen* revered Greek physician, author of a major medical text; *heart of
elder* i.e., fearful, cowardly: the elder tree has soft wood in its center, unlike
"heart of oak"; *stale* (1) urine (doctors diagnosed illness by examining patients' urine: see also l. 30, *King Urinal*, and ll. 51–52, *Monsieur Mockwater*),
(2) dupe, fool   30 *Castalion King Urinal* (invented insults: *Castalion* may
refer to [1] the spring of the Muses on Mount Parnassus, leading associa-
tively to the physician's urinal, the collecting beaker; or [2] Castiglione, Italian author of *The Courtier,* so that Caius is ironically prince of the learned
doctors; alternatively, *Castalion* may be an error for "Castilian" – i.e.,
Spaniard, another jingoistic insult)   30–31 *Hector of Greece* (jumbled name
for a heroic warrior: Hector was a Trojan)   36 *against the hair* i.e., the wrong
way ("against the grain")   39 *man of peace* nonfighter (but with play on
Shallow as justice of the peace)   40 *Bodykins* (mild oath: "God's little body")
42 *make one* join in (the fight)   43 *salt* i.e., flavor

51 HOST   Pardon, Guest Justice. A word, Monsieur Mockwater.

CAIUS   Mockvater? vat is dat?

HOST   Mockwater, in our English tongue, is valor, bully.

CAIUS   By gar, then I have as much mockvater as de Englishman. – Scurvy jack-dog priest! By gar, me vill cut
his ears.

58 HOST   He will clapperclaw thee titely, bully.

CAIUS   Clapper-de-claw? vat is dat?

60 HOST   That is, he will make thee amends.

CAIUS   By gar, me do look he shall clapper-de-claw me;
for, by gar, me vill have it.

63 HOST   And I will provoke him to't, or let him wag.

CAIUS   Me tank you for dat.

HOST   And moreover, bully – *[Aside]* But first, Master
Guest, and Master Page, and eke Cavaliero Slender, go

67 you through the town to Frogmore.

PAGE   Sir Hugh is there, is he?

HOST   He is there; see what humor he is in. And I will

70 bring the doctor about by the fields. Will it do well?

SHALLOW   We will do it.

PAGE, SHALLOW, SLENDER   Adieu, good Master Doctor.

            [Exeunt Page, Shallow, and Slender.]

CAIUS   By gar, me vill kill de priest, for he speak for a

74 jackanape to Anne Page.

HOST   Let him die. Sheathe thy impatience; throw cold

76 water on thy choler. Go about the fields with me
through Frogmore. I will bring thee where Mistress
Anne Page is, at a farmhouse a-feasting; and thou shalt

79 woo her. Cried game; said I well?

---

51 *Guest Justice* (Shallow, visiting from Gloucestershire, is perhaps the Host's guest at the Garter)   51–52 *Monsieur Mockwater* (another invented title concerning urinalysis, perhaps with pun on "make water")   58 *clapperclaw* thrash; *titely* quickly, smartly   63 *wag* depart (i.e., go to the devil)   67 *Frogmore* a village near Windsor   70 *about by* roundabout through   74 *jackanape* monkey, fool (i.e., Slender)   76 *choler* anger   79 *Cried game* (unexplained hunter's shout: perhaps "The quarry is sighted" or "The sport is proclaimed")

CAIUS   By gar, me dank you vor dat. By gar, I love you;   80
and I shall procure-a you de good guest – de earl, de
knight, de lords, de gentlemen, my patients.

HOST   For the which I will be thy adversary toward Anne   83
Page. Said I well?

CAIUS   By gar, 'tis good; vell said.

HOST   Let us wag, then.

CAIUS   Come at my heels, Jack Rugby.   *Exeunt.*
                    *

∾ **III.1** *Enter Evans, [and] Simple.*

EVANS   I pray you now, good Master Slender's servingman, and friend Simple by your name, which way have
you looked for Master Caius, that calls himself Doctor
of Physic?   4

SIMPLE   Marry, sir, the pittie-ward, the park-ward, every   5
way; Old Windsor way, and every way but the town
way.

EVANS   I most fehemently desire you, you will also look
that way.

SIMPLE   I will, sir.   *[Exit.]*   10

EVANS   Jeshu pless my soul, how full of cholers I am, and   11
trempling of mind. I shall be glad if he have deceived
me. How melancholies I am! I will knog his urinals   13
about his knave's costard when I have good opportuni-   14
ties for the 'ork. 'Pless my soul.
    [Sings.]
          "To shallow rivers, to whose falls   16
          Melodious birds sings madrigals;

---

83 *adversary* (supposedly "advocate," but the Host is still pulling Caius's leg)
    III.1 A field near Frogmore   4 *Physic* medicine (origin of "physician")   5
the pittie-ward toward Windsor Petty (Little) Park; *the park-ward* toward
Windsor Great Park   11 *cholers* (usually "anger," but Evans seems to be filled
with black choler, causing depression or melancholy, l. 13)   13 *knog* knock;
urinals i.e., private parts (or perhaps the collecting beaker)   14 *costard* head
(literally, a kind of apple)   16–19 *To shallow . . . posies* (a confused version of
Marlowe's "The Passionate Shepherd to His Love," beginning "Come live
with me, and be my love")

There will we make our peds of roses,
And a thousand fragrant posies.
20   To shallow –"

Mercy on me, I have a great dispositions to cry.
[Sings.]
     "Melodious birds sing madrigals –
23   Whenas I sat in Pabylon –
24   And a thousand vagram posies.
     To shallow –"

[Enter Simple.]
SIMPLE   Yonder he is coming, this way, Sir Hugh.
EVANS   He's welcome.
     [Sings.]
     "To shallow rivers, to whose falls –"

Heaven prosper the right! What weapons is he?
30 SIMPLE   No weapons, sir. There comes my master, Master Shallow, and another gentleman, from Frogmore,
32   over the stile, this way.
EVANS   Pray you, give me my gown, or else keep it in your arms.
     [Reading a book]
     [Enter] Page, Shallow, [and] Slender.
SHALLOW   How now, Master Parson? Good morrow,
36   good Sir Hugh. Keep a gamester from the dice, and a good student from his book, and it is wonderful.
SLENDER   *[Aside]* Ah sweet Anne Page!
PAGE   God save you, good Sir Hugh.
40 EVANS   God pless you from his mercy sake, all of you.
SHALLOW   What, the sword and the Word? Do you study them both, Master Parson?

---

23 *Whenas . . . Pabylon* (a line from Psalm 137)   24 *vagram* (error for "fragrant")   32 *stile* steps over a fence   36–37 *Keep . . . wonderful* i.e., a good student can't be kept from reading, no more than a gambler from betting

PAGE   And youthful still – in your doublet and hose this   43
     raw rheumatic day?   44

EVANS   There is reasons and causes for it.

PAGE   We are come to you to do a good office, Master
     Parson.

EVANS   Fery well; what is it?

PAGE   Yonder is a most reverend gentleman who, belike
     having received wrong by some person, is at most odds   50
     with his own gravity and patience that ever you saw.

SHALLOW   I have lived fourscore years and upward; I
     never heard a man of his place, gravity, and learning so
     wide of his own respect.   54

EVANS   What is he?

PAGE   I think you know him: Master Doctor Caius, the
     renowned French physician.

EVANS   Got's will, and his passion of my heart! I had as   58
     lief you would tell me of a mess of porridge.

PAGE   Why?   60

EVANS   He has no more knowledge in Hibocrates and   61
     Galen – and he is a knave besides, a cowardly knave as
     you would desires to be acquainted withal.

PAGE   I warrant you, he's the man should fight with him.

SLENDER   *[Aside]* O sweet Anne Page!

SHALLOW   It appears so by his weapons. Keep them
     asunder; here comes Doctor Caius.

     [Enter] Host, Caius, [and] Rugby.

PAGE   Nay, good Master Parson, keep in your weapon.

SHALLOW   So do you, good Master Doctor.

HOST   Disarm them, and let them question. Let them   70
     keep their limbs whole and hack our English.

---

43 *doublet and hose* close-fitting jacket and breeches (Evans is without his
cloak, which Simple holds)   44 *raw rheumatic* cold, causing illness   50–51
at odds . . . patience i.e., furious and undignified (*gravity* = seriousness)   54
wide . . . respect beside himself   58–59 *had as lief* would prefer   61–62 *Hibocrates and Galen* famous ancient Greek physicians (the first is Evans's mispronunciation of "Hippocrates," father of the Hippocratic oath)   70
question debate

CAIUS   I pray you let-a me speak a word with your ear.
73   Verefore vill you not meet-a me?

EVANS   *[Aside to Caius]* Pray you use your patience.
75   *[Aloud]* In good time.

CAIUS   By gar, you are de coward, de jack dog, John ape.

EVANS   *[Aside to Caius]* Pray you let us not be laughing-stocks to other men's humors. I desire you in friend-ship, and I will one way or other make you amends.
80   *[Aloud]* By Jeshu, I will knog your urinal about your
81   knave's cogscomb for missing your meetings and ap-pointments.

83   CAIUS   *Diable!* – Jack Rugby – mine host de Jarteer – have I not stay for him to kill him? Have I not, at de place I did appoint?

EVANS   As I am a Christians soul, now, look you, this is the place appointed. I'll be judgment by mine host of the Garter.

89   HOST   Peace, I say, Gallia and Gaul, French and Welsh,
90   soul curer and body curer.

CAIUS   Ay, dat is very good, excellent.

HOST   Peace, I say. Hear mine host of the Garter. Am I
93   politic? am I subtle? am I a Machiavel? Shall I lose my
94   doctor? No; he gives me the potions and the motions. Shall I lose my parson, my priest, my Sir Hugh? No; he
96   gives me the proverbs and the no-verbs. Give me thy
97   hand, terrestrial; so. Give me thy hand, celestial; so.
98   Boys of art, I have deceived you both; I have directed you to wrong places. Your hearts are mighty, your skins
100   are whole, and let burned sack be the issue. Come, lay

---

73 *Verefore* i.e., "wherefore," why   75 *In good time* at the proper moment
81 *cogscomb* coxcomb (fool's head)   83 *Diable* devil (French)   89 *Gallia and Gaul* (both words mean "France," although clearly the Host intends Wales and France; in French, "Pays de Galles" = Wales)   93 *politic* crafty (also "diplomatic"); *Machiavel* political intriguer, after Niccolò Machiavelli, author of *The Prince*   94 *motions* i.e., herbal laxatives causing "motion" of the bowels   96 *no-verbs* (Host's jab at Evans's language, to match *proverbs*) 97 *terrestrial . . . celestial* (doctors of the body and the soul)   98 *art* learning 100 *burned sack* warmed Spanish wine; *issue* conclusion   100–1 *Come . . . pawn* i.e., get rid of the weapons

their swords to pawn. Follow me, lads of peace; follow,
follow, follow.

SHALLOW   Afore God, a mad host. Follow, gentlemen,
follow.

SLENDER   *[Aside]* O sweet Anne Page!

> *[Exeunt Shallow, Slender, Page, and Host.]*

CAIUS   Ha, do I perceive dat? Have you make-a de sot of   106
us, ha, ha?

EVANS   This is well; he has made us his vloutingstog. I   108
desire you that we may be friends, and let us knog our
prains together to be revenge on this same scall, scurvy,   110
cogging companion, the host of the Garter.   111

CAIUS   By gar, with all my heart. He promise to bring me
where is Anne Page. By gar, he deceive me too.

EVANS   Well, I will smite his noddles. Pray you follow.   114

> *[Exeunt.]*

*

❧ **III.2**   *[Enter] Mistress Page, [and] Robin.*

MRS. PAGE   Nay, keep your way, little gallant: you were
wont to be a follower, but now you are a leader.   2
Whether had you rather, lead mine eyes or eye your   3
master's heels?

ROBIN   I had rather, forsooth, go before you like a man   5
than follow him like a dwarf.

MRS. PAGE   O, you are a flattering boy. Now I see you'll
be a courtier.

[Enter] Ford.

FORD   Well met, Mistress Page. Whither go you?

MRS. PAGE   Truly, sir, to see your wife. Is she at home?   10

---

106 *sot* fool   108 *vloutingstog* floutingstock (i.e., laughingstock)   110 *scall,
scurvy* i.e., diseased ("scald" = afflicted with scabs on the scalp)   111 *cogging*
cheating   114 *noddles* i.e., noddle, head

III.2 A street in Windsor   2 *wont* accustomed   3 *Whether . . . rather*
which would you prefer   5 *go . . . man* (possible sexual wordplay, for which
Mrs. Page jokingly reprimands him: *you'll be a courtier*)

11 FORD   Ay, and as idle as she may hang together, for want
12   of company. I think if your husbands were dead, you
  two would marry.

MRS. PAGE   Be sure of that — two other husbands.

15 FORD   Where had you this pretty weathercock?

16 MRS. PAGE   I cannot tell what the dickens his name is my
  husband had him of. What do you call your knight's
  name, sirrah?

ROBIN   Sir John Falstaff.

20 FORD   Sir John Falstaff!

MRS. PAGE   He, he; I can never hit on's name. There is
22   such a league between my goodman and he. Is your
  wife at home indeed?

FORD   Indeed she is.

25 MRS. PAGE   By your leave, sir. I am sick till I see her.

                 [Exeunt Mistress Page and Robin.]

FORD   Has Page any brains? hath he any eyes? hath he
  any thinking? Sure, they sleep; he hath no use of them.
  Why, this boy will carry a letter twenty mile as easy as a
29   cannon will shoot point-blank twelve score. He pieces
30   out his wife's inclination; he gives her folly motion and
  advantage; and now she's going to my wife, and Fal-
32   staff's boy with her. A man may hear this shower sing
  in the wind. And Falstaff's boy with her. Good plots!
  They are laid, and our revolted wives share damna-
  tion together. Well, I will take him, then torture my
  wife, pluck the borrowed veil of modesty from the so-
  seeming Mistress Page, divulge Page himself for a se-
38   cure and willful Actaeon; and to these violent

---

11 *as idle ... together* i.e., as bored as she can be   12–13 *you ... marry* i.e.,
each other   15 *pretty weathercock* inconstant little fellow   16 *what the dickens* what the devil (euphemism) 16–17 *his name ... of* i.e., the person who
sent him to my husband (Mistress Page is pretending ignorance)   22 *league*
friendly relationship   25 *sick till I* i.e., longing to   29 *shoot ... score* i.e., hit
a target at 240 paces   29–30 *pieces out* adds to (i.e., encourages; metaphor
from sewing)   30 *motion* advancement   32–33 *hear ... wind* anticipate the
rainstorm by the sound of the wind   38 *Actaeon* wearer of horns (i.e., victim; see II.1.108–9 n.)

proceedings all my neighbors shall cry "Aim!" *[Clock* 39
strikes.] The clock gives me my cue, and my assurance 40
bids me search. There I shall find Falstaff. I shall be
rather praised for this than mocked, for it is as positive
as the earth is firm that Falstaff is there. I will go.
   [Enter] Page, Shallow, Slender, Host, [Sir Hugh]
   Evans, Caius [, and Rugby].

SHALLOW, PAGE, ETC.   Well met, Master Ford.

FORD   Trust me, a good knot. I have good cheer at 45
home, and I pray you all go with me.

SHALLOW   I must excuse myself, Master Ford.

SLENDER   And so must I, sir. We have appointed to dine
with Mistress Anne, and I would not break with her for 49
more money than I'll speak of. 50

SHALLOW   We have lingered about a match between 51
Anne Page and my cousin Slender, and this day we shall
have our answer.

SLENDER   I hope I have your good will, father Page.

PAGE   You have, Master Slender. I stand wholly for you.
But my wife, Master Doctor, is for you altogether.

CAIUS   Ay, by gar, and de maid is love-a me. My nursh-a
Quickly tell me so mush.

HOST   What say you to young Master Fenton? He ca-
pers, he dances, he has eyes of youth, he writes verses, 60
he speaks holiday, he smells April and May. He will car- 61
ry't, he will carry't; 'tis in his buttons; he will carry't. 62

PAGE   Not by my consent, I promise you. The gentleman
is of no having. He kept company with the wild prince 64
and Poins; he is of too high a region; he knows too 65
much. No, he shall not knit a knot in his fortunes with 66
the finger of my substance. If he take her, let him take

---

39 *cry "Aim!"* shout encouragement (from archery) 45 *knot* group 49
break with her stand her up 51 *lingered* i.e., remained in Windsor 61
speaks holiday uses fancy language 61–62 *carry't* carry it off, succeed 62
'tis . . . buttons i.e., it's certain (the metaphor is unclear; perhaps *buttons* =
blossoms about to flower) 64 *of no having* i.e., broke 64–65 *wild . . .
Poins* (Prince Hal and his friend Poins in *1* and *2 Henry IV*) 65 *region* i.e.,
social class 66 *knit a knot in* mend

68 her simply. The wealth I have waits on my consent, and
    my consent goes not that way.
70 FORD   I beseech you heartily, some of you go home with
71 me to dinner. Besides your cheer, you shall have sport: I
72 will show you a monster. Master Doctor, you shall go.
    So shall you, Master Page, and you, Sir Hugh.
    SHALLOW   Well, fare you well. We shall have the freer
    wooing at Master Page's. *[Exeunt Shallow and Slender.]*
76 CAIUS   Go home, John Rugby. I come anon.
                                        [Exit Rugby.]
    HOST   Farewell, my hearts. I will to my honest knight
78 Falstaff, and drink canary with him.   *[Exit.]*
79 FORD   *[Aside]* I think I shall drink in pipe wine first with
80 him: I'll make him dance. — Will you go, gentles?
81 ALL   Have with you to see this monster.   *Exeunt.*

*

~ **III.3**   *Enter Mistress Ford, [and] Mistress Page.*

1 MRS. FORD   What, John! what, Robert!
2 MRS. PAGE   Quickly, quickly. — Is the buck basket —
   MRS. FORD   I warrant. What, Robert, I say!
   [Enter] Servants [with a basket].
   MRS. PAGE   Come, come, come.
   MRS. FORD   Here, set it down.
6 MRS. PAGE   Give your men the charge. We must be brief.
   MRS. FORD   Marry, as I told you before, John and
8 Robert, be ready here hard by in the brewhouse; and
   when I suddenly call you, come forth, and without any

---

68 *simply* alone (i.e., without a dowry)   71 *cheer* refreshments, food; *sport*
entertainment   72 *monster* rarity, freak (either the grotesque lover Falstaff or
the horned Master Page)   76 *anon* soon, right away   78 *canary* sweet wine
from the Canary Islands   79 *pipe wine* (1) wine from the cask (pipe), (2) in-
toxicating music from a flute (pipe): the sense is that Ford will call the tune
81 *Have with you* i.e., let's go
    III.3 Inside the Fords' house   1 *What* i.e., Hey! Get with it!   2 *buck bas-*
ket dirty-laundry (linen) basket (to *buck* clothing = to soak it)   6 *the charge*
instructions   8 *hard by* at hand

pause or staggering, take this basket on your shoulders. 10
That done, trudge with it in all haste, and carry it
among the whitsters in Datchet Mead, and there empty 12
it in the muddy ditch, close by the Thames side.

MRS. PAGE   You will do it?

MRS. FORD   I ha' told them over and over – they lack no
direction. Be gone, and come when you are called.

[Exeunt Servants.]

[Enter] Robin.

MRS. PAGE   Here comes little Robin.

MRS. FORD   How now, my eyas musket, what news with 18
you?

ROBIN   My master, Sir John, is come in at your back 20
door, Mistress Ford, and requests your company.

MRS. PAGE   You little Jack-a-Lent, have you been true 22
to us?

ROBIN   Ay, I'll be sworn. My master knows not of your
being here, and hath threatened to put me into everlasting liberty if I tell you of it; for he swears he'll turn
me away.

MRS. PAGE   Thou'rt a good boy. This secrecy of thine
shall be a tailor to thee and shall make thee a new dou- 29
blet and hose. I'll go hide me. 30

MRS. FORD   Do so. – Go tell thy master I am alone. *[Exit
Robin.]* Mistress Page, remember you your cue.

MRS. PAGE   I warrant thee. If I do not act it, hiss me.

[Exit.]

MRS. FORD   Go to, then. We'll use this unwholesome hu-
midity, this gross watery pumpkin – we'll teach him to
know turtles from jays. 36

[Enter] Falstaff.

---

12 *whitsters* bleachers of linen; *Datchet Mead* a meadow on the Thames near
Windsor   18 *eyas musket* young male sparrow hawk (figuratively, a lively
boy)   22 *Jack-a-Lent* puppet (from dummy figure made for games during
Lent)   29 *be a tailor to thee* earn you money for new clothes   36 *turtles from
jays* faithful turtledoves from flashy, promiscuous jaybirds (i.e., loose
women)

37 FALSTAFF "Have I caught thee, my heavenly jewel?"
    Why, now let me die, for I have lived long enough.
39 This is the period of my ambition. O this blessed hour!
40 MRS. FORD O sweet Sir John!
41 FALSTAFF Mistress Ford, I cannot cog, I cannot prate,
    Mistress Ford. Now shall I sin in my wish: I would thy
    husband were dead. I'll speak it before the best lord, I
    would make thee my lady.
    MRS. FORD I your lady, Sir John? Alas, I should be a piti-
    ful lady.
    FALSTAFF Let the court of France show me such another.
    I see how thine eye would emulate the diamond. Thou
49 hast the right arched beauty of the brow that becomes
50 the ship tire, the tire valiant, or any tire of Venetian ad-
    mittance.
    MRS. FORD A plain kerchief, Sir John – my brows be-
    come nothing else, nor that well neither.
    FALSTAFF By the Lord, thou art a tyrant to say so. Thou
55 wouldst make an absolute courtier, and the firm fixture
    of thy foot would give an excellent motion to thy gait
57 in a semicircled farthingale. I see what thou wert if For-
    tune thy foe were (not Nature) thy friend. Come, thou
    canst not hide it.
60 MRS. FORD Believe me, there's no such thing in me.
    FALSTAFF What made me love thee? Let that persuade
    thee there's something extraordinary in thee. Come, I
    cannot cog and say thou art this and that, like a many
64 of these lisping hawthorn buds that come like women

---

37 *Have I . . . jewel* (line, slightly altered, from Sidney's cycle of love sonnets, *Astrophil and Stella*) 39 *period* conclusion, achievement 41 *cog* deceive, flatter 49–50 *becomes the ship tire* shows off a headdress (*tire,* from "attire") in the form of a ship 50 *tire valiant* splendid headdress 50–51 *of Venetian admittance* allowed in Venice (center of fashion) 55 *an absolute* a perfect 55–56 *fixture . . . gait* i.e., your sure step will show off your walk especially well 57 *semicircled farthingale* petticoat with hoops not joined in front 57–58 *I see . . . friend* i.e., I can see that you would easily pass as an aristocrat if you had been favored not merely by Nature, responsible for beauty, but by Fortune, responsible for status ("Fortune My Foe" was a popular song) 64 *hawthorn buds* i.e., young dandies at court

in men's apparel and smell like Bucklersbury in simple   65
time. I cannot. But I love thee, none but thee; and thou
deservest it.

MRS. FORD   Do not betray me, sir. I fear you love Mis-   68
tress Page.

FALSTAFF   Thou mightst as well say I love to walk by the   70
Counter gate, which is as hateful to me as the reek of a   71
limekiln.

MRS. FORD   Well, heaven knows how I love you, and you
shall one day find it.

FALSTAFF   Keep in that mind; I'll deserve it.

MRS. FORD   Nay, I must tell you, so you do, or else I
could not be in that mind.

   [Enter Robin.]

ROBIN   Mistress Ford, Mistress Ford! Here's Mistress
Page at the door, sweating and blowing and looking
wildly, and would needs speak with you presently.   80

FALSTAFF   She shall not see me; I will ensconce me be-   81
hind the arras.   82

MRS. FORD   Pray you, do so: she's a very tattling woman.
   [Falstaff hides himself. Enter Mistress Page.]
What's the matter? how now?

MRS. PAGE   O Mistress Ford, what have you done? You're
shamed, you're overthrown, you're undone forever!

MRS. FORD   What's the matter, good Mistress Page?

MRS. PAGE   O welladay, Mistress Ford, having an honest   88
man to your husband, to give him such cause of suspicion!   90

MRS. FORD   What cause of suspicion?

MRS. PAGE   What cause of suspicion! Out upon you, how   92
am I mistook in you!

MRS. FORD   Why, alas, what's the matter?

---

65 *Bucklersbury* a London street where herbalists' shops were located   65–
66 *simple time* midsummer, when herbs were abundant and fragrant ("simples" = medicinal herbs)   68 *betray* deceive   71 *Counter* London debtors'
prison (notoriously dirty and smelly)   71–72 *a limekiln* an oven for producing powdered lime from limestone   81 *ensconce me* conceal myself securely
82 *arras* hanging tapestry   88 *welladay* alas   92 *Out upon* shame on

MRS. PAGE   Your husband's coming hither, woman, with
all the officers in Windsor, to search for a gentleman
that he says is here now in the house by your consent,
to take an ill advantage of his absence. You are undone.

MRS. FORD   'Tis not so, I hope.

100   MRS. PAGE   Pray heaven it be not so, that you have such a
man here! But 'tis most certain your husband's coming,
with half Windsor at his heels, to search for such a one.

103   I come before to tell you. If you know yourself clear,
104   why, I am glad of it; but if you have a friend here, con-
105   vey, convey him out. Be not amazed, call all your senses
to you, defend your reputation or bid farewell to your
good life forever.

108   MRS. FORD   What shall I do? There is a gentleman, my
dear friend; and I fear not mine own shame so much as
110   his peril. I had rather than a thousand pound he were
out of the house.

112   MRS. PAGE   For shame! Never stand "you had rather" and
"you had rather." Your husband's here at hand; bethink
you of some conveyance. In the house you cannot hide
him. O, how have you deceived me! Look, here is a basket. If he be of any reasonable stature, he may creep in
here; and throw foul linen upon him, as if it were going
118   to bucking. Or – it is whiting time – send him by your
two men to Datchet Mead.

120   MRS. FORD   He's too big to go in there. What shall I do?

FALSTAFF   *[Coming forward]* Let me see't, let me see't,
O let me see't! I'll in, I'll in. Follow your friend's counsel. I'll in.

MRS. PAGE   What, Sir John Falstaff! *[Aside]* Are these
your letters, knight?

FALSTAFF   *[Aside]* I love thee. Help me away. Let me
creep in here. I'll never –

---

103 *clear* innocent   104 *friend* i.e., lover   105 *amazed* puzzled, as if in a
maze   108–9 *my dear friend* (the phrase may be addressed to Mrs. Page or
may refer to Falstaff)   112 *stand* i.e., waste time ("stand around saying")
118 *bucking* washing

*[Gets into the basket; they cover him with dirty
laundry.]*

MRS. PAGE   Help to cover your master, boy. Call your
men, Mistress Ford. *[Aside]* You dissembling knight!   129

MRS. FORD   What, John! Robert! John!   *[Exit Robin.]*   130
[Enter Servants.]
Go take up these clothes here quickly. Where's the
cowlstaff? Look how you drumble! Carry them to the   132
laundress in Datchet Mead – quickly, come!
[Enter] Ford, Page, Caius, [and] Evans.

FORD   Pray you come near. If I suspect without cause,
why then make sport at me; then let me be your jest; I
deserve it. How now, whither bear you this?

SERVANTS   To the laundress, forsooth.

MRS. FORD   Why, what have you to do whither they bear   138
it? You were best meddle with buckwashing!

FORD   Buck? I would I could wash myself of the buck!   140
Buck, buck, buck! Ay, buck; I warrant you, buck; and
of the season too, it shall appear. *[Exeunt Servants with*   142
the basket.] Gentlemen, I have dreamed tonight; I'll tell   143
you my dream. Here, here, here be my keys. Ascend my
chambers; search, seek, find out. I'll warrant we'll un-   145
kennel the fox. Let me stop this way first. *[Locks the
door.]* So, now uncape.   147

PAGE   Good Master Ford, be contented. You wrong
yourself too much.

FORD   True, Master Page. Up, gentlemen; you shall see   150
sport anon. Follow me, gentlemen.   *[Exit.]*   151

EVANS   This is fery fantastical humors and jealousies.

---

129 *dissembling* deceiving   132 *cowlstaff* pole passed through handles of a
basket or tub (cowl) and carried by two men on their shoulders; *drumble*
move sluggishly, dawdle   138 *what . . . do* i.e., "What's it to you?"   140
Buck (Ford is obsessed with the horned beast, symbol of the cuckold)   142
season rutting season, when horns are most fully developed   143 *tonight* this
night (i.e., last night)   145–46 *unkennel* drive into the open   147 *uncape*
uncover (i.e., reveal yourself [?]: proposed emendations include "escape" and
"uncase")   151 *anon* shortly

CAIUS   By gar, 'tis no the fashion of France; it is not jealous in France.

PAGE   Nay, follow him, gentlemen – see the issue of his
search.   *[Exeunt Page, Caius, and Evans.]*

MRS. PAGE   Is there not a double excellency in this?

MRS. FORD   I know not which pleases me better: that my
husband is deceived, or Sir John.

160   MRS. PAGE   What a taking was he in when your husband
asked what was in the basket!

162   MRS. FORD   I am half afraid he will have need of washing; so throwing him into the water will do him a
benefit.

MRS. PAGE   Hang him, dishonest rascal! I would all of the
same strain were in the same distress.

MRS. FORD   I think my husband hath some special suspicion of Falstaff's being here, for I never saw him so
gross in his jealousy till now.

170   MRS. PAGE   I will lay a plot to try that, and we will yet
have more tricks with Falstaff – his dissolute disease
172   will scarce obey this medicine.

173   MRS. FORD   Shall we send that foolish carrion Mistress
174   Quickly to him, and excuse his throwing into the
water; and give him another hope, to betray him to another punishment?

MRS. PAGE   We will do it. Let him be sent for tomorrow
eight o'clock, to have amends.

[Enter Ford, Page, Caius, and Evans.]

179   FORD   I cannot find him. Maybe the knave bragged of
180   that he could not compass.

MRS. PAGE   *[Aside to Mistress Ford]* Heard you that?

MRS. FORD   You use me well, Master Ford, do you?

FORD   Ay, I do so.

MRS. FORD   Heaven make you better than your thoughts!

---

160 *taking* state (of terror)   162–63 *he . . . washing* i.e., he will have soiled
himself in fear   170 *try* test   172 *obey* respond to   173 *carrion* (term for
aging flesh, with a pun on "carry"?)   174 *excuse his throwing* i.e., make ex-
cuses for his having been thrown   179–80 *bragged . . . compass* boasted
about something he couldn't achieve

FORD Amen.

MRS. PAGE   You do yourself mighty wrong, Master Ford.

FORD   Ay, ay, I must bear it.

EVANS   If there be any pody in the house, and in the
chambers, and in the coffers, and in the presses, heaven 189
forgive my sins at the day of judgment. 190

CAIUS   By gar, nor I too, there is nobodies.

PAGE   Fie, fie, Master Ford, are you not ashamed? What
spirit, what devil suggests this imagination? I would 193
not ha' your distemper in this kind for the wealth of 194
Windsor Castle.

FORD   'Tis my fault, Master Page. I suffer for it.

EVANS   You suffer for a pad conscience. Your wife is as
honest a 'omans as I will desires among five thousand,
and five hundred too.

CAIUS   By gar, I see 'tis an honest woman. 200

FORD   Well, I promised you a dinner. Come, come, walk
in the park. I pray you pardon me. I will hereafter make
known to you why I have done this. Come, wife; come,
Mistress Page. I pray you pardon me; pray heartily pardon me.

PAGE   Let's go in, gentlemen; but, trust me, we'll mock
him. I do invite you tomorrow morning to my house to
breakfast. After, we'll a-birding together: I have a fine 208
hawk for the bush. Shall it be so? 209

FORD   Anything. 210

EVANS   If there is one, I shall make two in the company. 211

CAIUS   If there be one, or two, I shall make-a the turd.

FORD   Pray you go, Master Page.

---

189 *coffers* storage chests; *presses* cupboards   193 *imagination* delusion, fantasy   194 *your distemper . . . kind* i.e., the sort of unstable mental condition
you display   208 *a-birding* (here, hunting with hawks and guns)   209 *for
the bush* (the hawk drove the small birds into bushes, where the hunter could
shoot them more easily)   211 *make two* (error for "make one" – i.e., join the
group)

214 EVANS I pray you now, remembrance tomorrow on the
lousy knave, mine host.

CAIUS Dat is good; by gar, with all my heart.

EVANS A lousy knave, to have his gibes and his mock-
eries!   *Exeunt.*

*

∾ **III.4** *Enter Fenton, [and] Anne [Page].*

FENTON
I see I cannot get thy father's love;
2   Therefore no more turn me to him, sweet Nan.

ANNE
Alas, how then?

FENTON   Why, thou must be thyself.
He doth object I am too great of birth,
5   And that my state being galled with my expense,
I seek to heal it only by his wealth.
7   Besides these, other bars he lays before me,
8   My riots past, my wild societies;
And tells me 'tis a thing impossible
10 I should love thee but as a property.

ANNE
Maybe he tells you true.

FENTON
12 No, heaven so speed me in my time to come!
Albeit I will confess thy father's wealth
Was the first motive that I wooed thee, Anne,
Yet, wooing thee, I found thee of more value
16 Than stamps in gold or sums in sealèd bags;

214–15 *remembrance . . . host* (probably an attempt at "Don't forget what
we'll do to the host tomorrow," but *remembrance* may be an error for "revenge" and/or "vengeance")
III.4 Before the Pages' house **2** *turn* send **5** *state . . . expense* estate
being diseased or injured (*galled* = afflicted with sores) by my extravagance
7 *bars* obstacles **8** *wild societies* bad companionship **10** *property* means to
an end (with financial sense) **12** *heaven so . . . come* as I hope for salvation
16 *stamps* coins (stamped with an image)

And 'tis the very riches of thyself
That now I aim at.
ANNE   Gentle Master Fenton,
Yet seek my father's love; still seek it, sir.
If opportunity and humblest suit   20
Cannot attain it, why, then – hark you hither.   21
  [They talk apart.]
  [Enter] Shallow, Slender, [and Mistress] Quickly.
SHALLOW . Break their talk, Mistress Quickly. My kins-
man shall speak for himself.
SLENDER   I'll make a shaft or a bolt on't. 'Slid, 'tis but   24
venturing.
SHALLOW   Be not dismayed.   26
SLENDER   No, she shall not dismay me. I care not for
that, but that I am afeard.   28
QUICKLY   Hark ye, Master Slender would speak a word
with you.   30
ANNE
  I come to him. *[Aside]* This is my father's choice.
  O, what a world of vile ill-favored faults   32
  Looks handsome in three hundred pounds a year.
QUICKLY   And how does good Master Fenton? Pray you a
word with you.
SHALLOW   She's coming; to her, coz. O boy, thou hadst a   36
father!
SLENDER   I had a father, Mistress Anne – my uncle can
tell you good jests of him. Pray you, uncle, tell Mistress
Anne the jest how my father stole two geese out of a   40
pen, good uncle.
SHALLOW   Mistress Anne, my cousin loves you.

---

21 *hark you hither* i.e., follow me over here (as Shallow and company enter)
24 *I'll . . . on't* I'll try with a slender arrow or a thick one (i.e., one way or the
other; Slender's language is heavy with clichés); *'Slid* by God's eyelid   24–25
'tis but venturing i.e., What's to be lost?   26 *dismayed* frightened   28 *but . . .
afeard* i.e., except that I'm frightened (Slender is nervous and confused)   32
ill-favored ugly   36 *coz* i.e., cousin (term used for any relative; see l. 42)
36–37 *thou hadst a father* i.e., Go to her like a man!

SLENDER Ay, that I do, as well as I love any woman in
    Gloucestershire.

SHALLOW He will maintain you like a gentlewoman.

46 SLENDER Ay, that I will, come cut and longtail, under
    the degree of a squire.

SHALLOW He will make you a hundred and fifty pounds
49   jointure.

50 ANNE Good Master Shallow, let him woo for himself.

SHALLOW Marry, I thank you for it, I thank you for that
    good comfort. She calls you, coz. I'll leave you.

ANNE Now, Master Slender –

SLENDER Now, good Mistress Anne –

ANNE What is your will?

56 SLENDER My will? 'Od's heartlings, that's a pretty jest in-
    deed! I ne'er made my will yet, I thank God. I am not
    such a sickly creature, I give heaven praise.

ANNE I mean, Master Slender, what would you with me?

60 SLENDER Truly, for mine own part, I would little or
    nothing with you. Your father and my uncle have made
62   motions. If it be my luck, so; if not, happy man be his
    dole. They can tell you how things go better than I can.
    You may ask your father; here he comes.

    [Enter] Page, [and] Mistress Page.

PAGE
  Now, Master Slender. Love him, daughter Anne. –
  Why, how now, what does Master Fenton here?
  You wrong me, sir, thus still to haunt my house.
  I told you, sir, my daughter is disposed of.

FENTON
  Nay, Master Page, be not impatient.

46–47 *come . . . squire* i.e., you'll have every comfort that someone at the
rank of squire can provide (*cut and longtail,* referring to horses or dogs, was
proverbial for "everything"; cf. "the long and the short of it") 49 *jointure*
portion of husband's estate guaranteed the wife if he were to die 56 *'Od's
heartlings* by God's little heart (a mild oath); *pretty jest* (because the young
Slender has misread *will* as "will and testament") 62 *motions* offers, propos-
als 62–63 *happy . . . dole* i.e., happiness to whoever wins you (another conventional phrase)

MRS. PAGE
   Good Master Fenton, come not to my child.   70
PAGE
   She is no match for you.
FENTON
   Sir, will you hear me?
PAGE   No, good Master Fenton.
   Come, Master Shallow; come, son Slender, in.
   Knowing my mind, you wrong me, Master Fenton.
                    [Exeunt Page, Shallow, and Slender.]
QUICKLY   Speak to Mistress Page.
FENTON
   Good Mistress Page, for that I love your daughter   76
   In such a righteous fashion as I do,
   Perforce, against all checks, rebukes, and manners,   78
   I must advance the colors of my love   79
   And not retire. Let me have your good will.   80
ANNE   Good mother, do not marry me to yond fool.
MRS. PAGE   I mean it not. I seek you a better husband.
QUICKLY   *[Aside]* That's my master, Master Doctor.
ANNE
   Alas, I had rather be set quick i' th' earth,   84
   And bowled to death with turnips.
MRS. PAGE
   Come, trouble not yourself. Good Master Fenton,
   I will not be your friend, nor enemy.
   My daughter will I question how she loves you,
   And as I find her, so am I affected.
   Till then, farewell, sir. She must needs go in;   90
   Her father will be angry.
FENTON
   Farewell, gentle mistress. Farewell, Nan.
                    [Exeunt Mistress Page, and Anne.]

---

76 *for that* because   78 *against . . . manners* despite obstacles and conventions   79–80 *advance . . . retire* (military metaphor: Fenton's love is a flag
that must go forward, not retreat)   84 *set quick* buried alive (here, up to the
neck)

QUICKLY   This is my doing now. "Nay," said I, "will you cast away your child on a fool, and a physician? Look on Master Fenton." This is my doing.

FENTON

96 I thank thee, and I pray thee once tonight
97 Give my sweet Nan this ring. There's for thy pains.

QUICKLY   Now heaven send thee good fortune! *[Exit Fenton.]* A kind heart he hath. A woman would run
100 through fire and water for such a kind heart. But yet I would my master had Mistress Anne; or I would Master Slender had her; or, in sooth, I would Master Fenton had her. I will do what I can for them all three, for so I have promised, and I'll be as good as my word; but
105 speciously for Master Fenton. Well, I must of another errand to Sir John Falstaff from my two mistresses. What a beast am I to slack it!   *[Exit.]*

*

∾ **III.5** *Enter Falstaff, [and] Bardolph.*

FALSTAFF   Bardolph, I say.

BARDOLPH   Here, sir.

3 FALSTAFF   Go fetch me a quart of sack – put a toast in't. *[Exit Bardolph.]* Have I lived to be carried in a basket
5 like a barrow of butcher's offal? And to be thrown in the Thames! Well, if I be served such another trick, I'll have my brains ta'en out, and buttered, and give them
8 to a dog for a New Year's gift. 'Sblood, the rogues
9 slighted me into the river with as little remorse as they
10 would have drowned a blind bitch's puppies, fifteen i' the litter – and you may know by my size that I have a

96 *once* sometime   97 *pains* trouble (as Fenton tips her)   105 *speciously* (error for "especially"); *must of* i.e., must take care of

III.5 A room in the Garter Inn   3 *a toast* hot bread for sopping   5 *offal* discarded parts of butchered animals   8 *New Year's* (traditional day for gift giving, equivalent to modern Christmas); *'Sblood* (an oath; originally "by God's [i.e., Christ's] blood")   9 *slighted* (combination of "slight" ["treat badly"] and "slide"? Q reads "slided")

kind of alacrity in sinking; if the bottom were as deep
as hell, I should down. I had been drowned but that the
shore was shelvy and shallow – a death that I abhor, for   14
the water swells a man, and what a thing should I have
been when I had been swelled. I should have been a
mountain of mummy.   17
  [Enter Bardolph with wine.]
BARDOLPH   Here's Mistress Quickly, sir, to speak with
you.
FALSTAFF   Come, let me pour in some sack to the   20
Thames water, for my belly's as cold as if I had swal-
lowed snowballs for pills to cool the reins. Call her in.   22
BARDOLPH   Come in, woman.
  [Enter Mistress] Quickly.
QUICKLY   By your leave; I cry you mercy. Give your wor-   24
ship good morrow.
FALSTAFF   Take away these chalices. Go, brew me a pottle   26
of sack finely.
BARDOLPH   With eggs, sir?
FALSTAFF   Simple of itself. I'll no pullet sperm in my
brewage. *[Exit Bardolph.]* How now?   30
QUICKLY   Marry, sir, I come to your worship from Mis-
tress Ford.
FALSTAFF   Mistress Ford? I have had ford enough; I was   33
thrown into the ford; I have my belly full of ford.
QUICKLY   Alas the day, good heart, that was not her fault.
She does so take on with her men – they mistook their   36
erection.   37
FALSTAFF   So did I mine, to build upon a foolish woman's
promise.
QUICKLY   Well, she laments, sir, for it, that it would yearn   40
your heart to see it. Her husband goes this morning

---

14 *shore* river bottom near the edge   17 *mummy* dead flesh   22 *reins* kid-
neys   24 *cry you mercy* beg your pardon   26 *chalices* goblets   33 *ford* i.e., in
a river, a shallow spot for crossing   36 *take . . . men* reprimand her servants
37 *erection* (blunder for "direction," taken up by Falstaff in the next line)
40 *yearn* grieve

a-birding. She desires you once more to come to her between eight and nine. I must carry her word quickly.
She'll make you amends, I warrant you.

FALSTAFF Well, I will visit her, tell her so. And bid her
think what a man is: let her consider his frailty, and
then judge of my merit.

QUICKLY I will tell her.

FALSTAFF Do so. Between nine and ten, sayst thou?

50 QUICKLY Eight and nine, sir.

FALSTAFF Well, be gone. I will not miss her.

QUICKLY Peace be with you, sir.   *[Exit.]*

FALSTAFF I marvel I hear not of Master Brook. He sent
me word to stay within. I like his money well.
[Enter] Ford.
By the mass, here he comes.

FORD God save you, sir.

FALSTAFF Now, Master Brook, you come to know what
hath passed between me and Ford's wife?

FORD That, indeed, Sir John, is my business.

60 FALSTAFF Master Brook, I will not lie to you. I was at her
house the hour she appointed me.

62 FORD And sped you, sir?

63 FALSTAFF Very ill-favoredly, Master Brook.

64 FORD How so, sir? Did she change her determination?

65 FALSTAFF No, Master Brook, but the peaking cornuto
her husband, Master Brook, dwelling in a continual

67 'larum of jealousy, comes me in the instant of our en-

68 counter, after we had embraced, kissed, protested, and,
as it were, spoke the prologue of our comedy; and at his

70 heels a rabble of his companions, thither provoked and
instigated by his distemper, and, forsooth, to search his
house for his wife's love.

FORD What, while you were there?

---

62 *sped you* did you succeed, how did it go   63 *ill-favoredly* badly (literally,
"ill-favored" = ugly)   64 *determination* decision   65 *peaking cornuto* sneak-
ing cuckold (*cornuto* [Italian] = horned one)   67 *'larum* state of alarm   68
protested i.e., declared love for each other

FALSTAFF   While I was there.

FORD   And did he search for you, and could not find you?

FALSTAFF   You shall hear. As good luck would have it, comes in one Mistress Page, gives intelligence of Ford's approach, and in her invention, and Ford's wife's dis- traction, they conveyed me into a buck basket.   80

FORD   A buck basket?

FALSTAFF   By the Lord, a buck basket! Rammed me in with foul shirts and smocks, socks, foul stockings,   83 greasy napkins, that, Master Brook, there was the rank- est compound of villainous smell that ever offended nostril.

FORD   And how long lay you there?

FALSTAFF   Nay, you shall hear, Master Brook, what I have suffered to bring this woman to evil for your good. Being thus crammed in the basket, a couple of Ford's   90 knaves, his hinds, were called forth by their mistress to   91 carry me in the name of foul clothes to Datchet Lane. They took me on their shoulders, met the jealous knave their master in the door, who asked them once or twice what they had in their basket. I quaked for fear lest the lunatic knave would have searched it; but Fate, ordain- ing he should be a cuckold, held his hand. Well, on   97 went he for a search, and away went I for foul clothes. But mark the sequel, Master Brook. I suffered the pangs of three several deaths: first, an intolerable fright   100 to be detected with a jealous rotten bellwether; next, to   101 be compassed like a good bilbo in the circumference of   102 a peck, hilt to point, heel to head; and then, to be stopped in, like a strong distillation, with stinking   104 clothes that fretted in their own grease. Think of that, a   105

---

83 *smocks* linen undergarments   91 *hinds* servants (used contemptuously) 97 *held* stayed   100 *several* separate, different   101 *detected with* discovered by; *rotten bellwether* diseased old ram (wearing a bell, the *bellwether* leads the flock)   102–3 *compassed . . . peck* (bent like a flexible sword [*bilbo*] in a two- gallon basket)   104 *stopped in* stuffed, stoppered; *strong distillation* smelly liquid   105 *fretted* rotted

106 man of my kidney -- think of that -- that am as subject
107 to heat as butter; a man of continual dissolution and
     thaw. It was a miracle to scape suffocation. And in the
     height of this bath, when I was more than half stewed
110 in grease like a Dutch dish, to be thrown into the
     Thames, and cooled, glowing hot, in that surge, like a
     horseshoe. Think of that -- hissing hot -- think of that,
     Master Brook!

114 FORD   In good sadness, sir, I am sorry that for my sake
     you have suffered all this. My suit then is desperate.
     You'll undertake her no more?

117 FALSTAFF   Master Brook, I will be thrown into Etna, as I
     have been into Thames, ere I will leave her thus. Her
     husband is this morning gone a-birding. I have received
120 from her another embassy of meeting. Twixt eight and
     nine is the hour, Master Brook.

     FORD   'Tis past eight already, sir.

123 FALSTAFF   Is it? I will then address me to my appoint-
     ment. Come to me at your convenient leisure, and you
     shall know how I speed; and the conclusion shall be
     crowned with your enjoying her. Adieu. You shall have
     her, Master Brook; Master Brook, you shall cuckold
     Ford.   *[Exit.]*

     FORD   Hum, ha! is this a vision? is this a dream? do I
130 sleep? Master Ford, awake; awake, Master Ford! There's
131 a hole made in your best coat, Master Ford. This 'tis to
     be married; this 'tis to have linen and buck baskets!
     Well, I will proclaim myself what I am. I will now take
     the lecher. He is at my house, he cannot scape me, 'tis
     impossible he should. He cannot creep into a halfpenny
     purse, nor into a pepperbox, but lest the devil that
     guides him should aid him, I will search impossible
     places. Though what I am I cannot avoid, yet to be

---

106 *kidney* nature, makeup   107 *dissolution* dissolving   114 *sadness* seriousness   117 *Etna* a Sicilian volcano   120 *embassy* message   123 *address me to*
ready myself for   131 *hole . . . coat* (proverbial phrase for an unhappy discovery)

what I would not, shall not make me tame. If I have
horns to make one mad, let the proverb go with me: I'll   *140*
be horn-mad.   *[Exit.]*   141

                         *

∾ **IV.1** *Enter Mistress Page, [Mistress] Quickly, [and]
William.*

MRS. PAGE   Is he at Mistress Ford's already, think'st thou?
QUICKLY   Sure he is by this, or will be presently. But
   truly, he is very courageous mad about his throwing   3
   into the water. Mistress Ford desires you to come suddenly.
MRS. PAGE   I'll be with her by and by – I'll but bring my   6
   young man here to school. Look where his master
   comes; 'tis a playing day, I see.   8
   [Enter] Evans.
   How now, Sir Hugh, no school today?
EVANS   No. Master Slender is let the boys leave to play.   10
QUICKLY   'Blessing of his heart.
MRS. PAGE   Sir Hugh, my husband says my son profits   12
   nothing in the world at his book. I pray you, ask him
   some questions in his accidence.   14
EVANS   Come hither, William. Hold up your head;
   come.
MRS. PAGE   Come on, sirrah; hold up your head; answer
   your master, be not afraid.
EVANS   William, how many numbers is in nouns?   19
WILLIAM   Two.   20

---

141 *horn-mad* i.e., enraged, like the proverbial cuckolded husband
   IV.1 A street in Windsor   3 *courageous mad* furious (i.e., heartily angry;
or perhaps an error for "outrageously"?)   6 *by and by* very soon   8 *playing
day* holiday   10 *let . . . play* i.e., requested a holiday for the boys (so that
Evans can help with Slender's wooing?)   12–13 *profits . . . world* makes no
progress   14 *accidence* basics of Latin grammar (the standard text, from
which Evans's examples are taken, is Lily and Colet's *A Short Introduction of
[Latin] Grammar*, published 1543 and often reprinted)   19 *numbers* i.e.,
singular and plural

QUICKLY   Truly, I thought there had been one number
22   more, because they say "'Od's nouns."

EVANS   Peace your tattlings. What is "fair," William?

WILLIAM   *Pulcher.*

25 QUICKLY   Polecats! There are fairer things than polecats,
sure.

EVANS   You are a very simplicity 'oman. I pray you peace.
What is *lapis,* William?

WILLIAM   A stone.

30 EVANS   And what is "a stone," William?

WILLIAM   A pebble.

EVANS   No, it is *lapis.* I pray you remember in your
prain.

WILLIAM   *Lapis.*

EVANS   That is a good William. What is he, William,
that does lend articles?

WILLIAM   Articles are borrowed of the pronoun, and be
38   thus declined: *Singulariter, nominativo, hic, haec, hoc.*

39 EVANS   *Nominativo, hig, hag, hog.* Pray you mark: *geni-*
40   *tivo, hujus.* Well, what is your accusative case?

WILLIAM   *Accusativo, hinc.*

EVANS   I pray you, have your remembrance, child: *accusativo, hung, hang, hog.*

44 QUICKLY   "Hang-hog" is Latin for bacon, I warrant you.

45 EVANS   Leave your prabbles, 'oman. What is the focative
case, William?

WILLIAM   *O, vocativo, O.*

48 EVANS   Remember, William; focative is *caret.*

---

22 *'Od's nouns* (error for "God's [i.e., Christ's] wounds": by Quickly's logic,
the *nouns* would be three, an *odd* number)   25 *Polecats* (small animals of the
weasel family, different from the North American skunk; the first of
Quickly's many bawdy misconstructions in this scene: "polecat" is slang for
"prostitute")   38 *Singulariter, nominativo* in the singular, in the nominative;
hic, haec, hoc (forms of "this")   39 *hig, hag, hog* (Evans mispronounces
William's declension in the previous line; he does so again in l. 43); *mark* pay
attention   39–40 *genitivo* in the genitive case   44 *Hang-hog* (proverb: "Hog
is not bacon until it be hanged")   45 *focative* i.e., vocative   48 *caret* (Latin:
"it is lacking")

QUICKLY   And that's a good root.   49

EVANS   'Oman, forbear.   50

MRS. PAGE   Peace.

EVANS   What is your genitive case plural, William?

WILLIAM   Genitive case?

EVANS   Ay.

WILLIAM   *Genitivo, horum, harum, horum.*   55

QUICKLY   'Vengeance of Jenny's case! fie on her! Never   56
name her, child, if she be a whore.

EVANS   For shame, 'oman.

QUICKLY   You do ill to teach the child such words. He
teaches him to hick and to hack, which they'll do fast   60
enough of themselves, and to call "horum." Fie upon
you!

EVANS   'Oman, art thou lunatics? Hast thou no under-
standings for thy cases and the numbers of the genders?
Thou art as foolish Christian creatures as I would desires.

MRS. PAGE   *[To Mrs. Quickly]* Prithee hold thy peace.

EVANS   Show me now, William, some declensions of
your pronouns.

WILLIAM   Forsooth, I have forgot.   70

EVANS   It is *qui, quae, quod.* If you forget your *qui*'s, your   71
quae's, and your *quod*'s, you must be preeches. Go your   72
ways and play, go.

MRS. PAGE   He is a better scholar than I thought he was.

EVANS   He is a good sprag memory. Farewell, Mistress   75
Page.

---

49 *root* i.e., carrot (the sexual connotations multiply, with the mispronunciation of *focative* as "fuckative," Quickly's association of *caret* – "carrot" and
root – with "penis," and William's *O*, slang term for female sexual organs)   55
horum, harum, horum (William continues his declension of *hic,* but Quickly
hears "whore" and "hare" – i.e., prostitute)   56 *'Vengeance . . . case* God's
vengeance – i.e., a plague on (1) *Jenny's* vagina, (2) her pregnant condition
60 *hick* hiccup (i.e., drink); *hack* fuck (see also II.1.47)   71–72 *qui . . . quod*'s
(if Evans pronounces *qui*'s, *quae*'s, and *quod*'s as "keys, case, and cods," there
are further sexual undertones: "penis," "vagina," and "testicles")   72 *preeches*
i.e., breeched, whipped on the bare buttocks   75 *sprag* i.e., "sprack," lively

MRS. PAGE   Adieu, good Sir Hugh. *[Exit Evans.]* Get you
home, boy. Come, we stay too long.   *Exeunt.*

*

~ **IV.2**   *Enter Falstaff, [and] Mistress Ford.*

1   FALSTAFF   Mistress Ford, your sorrow hath eaten up my
2   sufferance. I see you are obsequious in your love, and I
3   profess requital to a hair's breadth, not only, Mistress
4   Ford, in the simple office of love, but in all the accou-
    trement, complement, and ceremony of it. But are you
    sure of your husband now?
    MRS. FORD   He's a-birding, sweet Sir John.
8   MRS. PAGE   *[Within]* What ho, gossip Ford! What ho!
    MRS. FORD   Step into the chamber, Sir John.
                                              [Exit Falstaff.]
        [Enter] Mistress Page.
10 MRS. PAGE   How now, sweetheart, who's at home besides
    yourself?
12 MRS. FORD   Why, none but mine own people.
    MRS. PAGE   Indeed?
    MRS. FORD   No, certainly. *[Aside to her]* Speak louder.
    MRS. PAGE   Truly, I am so glad you have nobody here.
    MRS. FORD   Why?
    MRS. PAGE   Why, woman, your husband is in his old
18 lunes again. He so takes on yonder with my husband;
    so rails against all married mankind; so curses all Eve's
20 daughters, of what complexion soever; and so buffets
21 himself on the forehead, crying "Peer out, peer out!"
    that any madness I ever yet beheld seemed but tame-

IV.2 A room in the Fords' house   1–2 *eaten . . . sufferance* i.e., dispelled or
made me forget my suffering   2 *obsequious* dutiful, eager to please   3 *profess . . . breadth* i.e., promise equivalent devotion   4–5 *accoutrement . . . ceremony* (three affected terms for the formalities of courtship)   8 *gossip* female
friend or neighbor   12 *people* i.e., household servants   18 *lunes* fits of lu-
nacy   20 *complexion* temperament   21 *Peer out* (addressed to his imaginary
cuckold's horns)

ness, civility, and patience to this his distemper he is in
now. I am glad the fat knight is not here.

MRS. FORD Why, does he talk of him?

MRS. PAGE Of none but him; and swears he was carried
out, the last time he searched for him, in a basket;
protests to my husband he is now here, and hath drawn
him and the rest of their company from their sport to
make another experiment of his suspicion. But I am *30*
glad the knight is not here. Now he shall see his own
foolery.

MRS. FORD How near is he, Mistress Page?

MRS. PAGE Hard by, at street end; he will be here anon.

MRS. FORD I am undone! The knight is here! *35*

MRS. PAGE Why then you are utterly shamed, and he's
but a dead man. What a woman are you! Away with
him, away with him! Better shame than murder.

MRS. FORD Which way should he go? How should I be- *39*
stow him? Shall I put him into the basket again? *40*

[Enter] Falstaff.

FALSTAFF No. I'll come no more i' the basket. May I not
go out ere he come?

MRS. PAGE Alas, three of Master Ford's brothers watch
the door with pistols that none shall issue out; otherwise you might slip away ere he came. But what make
you here?

FALSTAFF What shall I do? I'll creep up into the chimney.

MRS. FORD There they always use to discharge their *48*
birding pieces. *49*

MRS. PAGE Creep into the kilnhole. *50*

FALSTAFF Where is it?

MRS. FORD He will seek there, on my word. Neither
press, coffer, chest, trunk, well, vault, but he hath an *53*
abstract for the remembrance of such places, and goes

---

35 *undone* ruined 39–40 *How . . . bestow* where can I put 48 *use* are accustomed 49 *pieces* guns 50 *kilnhole* oven 53 *press* linen press (i.e., cup-
board) 53–54 *an abstract* a list

to them by his note. There is no hiding you in the house.

FALSTAFF   I'll go out, then.

MRS. PAGE   If you go out in your own semblance, you die, Sir John. Unless you go out disguised —

60 MRS. FORD   How might we disguise him?

MRS. PAGE   Alas the day, I know not. There is no woman's gown big enough for him; otherwise, he might put on a hat, a muffler, and a kerchief, and so escape.

FALSTAFF   Good hearts, devise something. Any extremity rather than a mischief.

67 MRS. FORD   My maid's aunt, the fat woman of Brainford, has a gown above.

MRS. PAGE   On my word, it will serve him; she's as big as

70 he is. And there's her thrummed hat and her muffler too. Run up, Sir John.

MRS. FORD   Go, go, sweet Sir John! Mistress Page and I will look some linen for your head.

74 MRS. PAGE   Quick, quick! We'll come dress you straight; put on the gown the while.   *[Exit Falstaff.]*

MRS. FORD   I would my husband would meet him in this shape. He cannot abide the old woman of Brainford; he swears she's a witch, forbade her my house, and hath threatened to beat her.

80 MRS. PAGE   Heaven guide him to thy husband's cudgel, and the devil guide his cudgel afterwards!

MRS. FORD   But is my husband coming?

83 MRS. PAGE   Ay, in good sadness, is he; and talks of the
84 basket too, howsoever he hath had intelligence.

85 MRS. FORD   We'll try that; for I'll appoint my men to carry the basket again, to meet him at the door with it, as they did last time.

---

67 *fat woman of Brainford* (possibly a historical person who kept a tavern at a village, now Brentford, downriver from Windsor)   70 *thrummed* fringed   74 *straight* straightaway, immediately   83 *good sadness* all seriousness   84 *howsoever . . . intelligence* i.e., which he somehow seems to have found out about   85 *try* test

MRS. PAGE   Nay, but he'll be here presently. Let's go dress
him like the witch of Brainford.

MRS. FORD   I'll first direct my men what they shall do   *90*
with the basket. Go up; I'll bring linen for him straight.
                                                          [Exit.]

MRS. PAGE   Hang him, dishonest varlet, we cannot mis-   *92*
use him enough.
        We'll leave a proof, by that which we will do,
        Wives may be merry, and yet honest too.
        We do not act, that often jest and laugh;
        'Tis old but true, "Still swine eats all the draff."   *97*
                                                          [Exit.]

[Enter Mistress Ford, with two] Servants.

MRS. FORD   Go, sirs, take the basket again on your shoulders. Your master is hard at door; if he bid you set it
down, obey him. Quickly, dispatch.   *[Exit.]*   *100*

FIRST SERVANT   Come, come, take it up.

SECOND SERVANT   Pray heaven it be not full of knight
again.

FIRST SERVANT   I hope not; I had as lief bear so much   *104*
lead.

[Enter] Ford, Page, Caius, Evans, [and] Shallow.

FORD   Ay, but if it prove true, Master Page, have you any   *106*
way then to unfool me again? Set down the basket, villains. Somebody call my wife. Youth in a basket! O you
panderly rascals! There's a knot, a gang, a pack, a con-   *109*
spiracy against me. Now shall the devil be shamed.   *110*
What, wife, I say! Come, come forth! Behold what
honest clothes you send forth to bleaching!

---

92 *dishonest varlet* lustful scoundrel   **97** *Still . . . draff* (proverbially, "The
silent pig eats more swill" – i.e., merry wives are innocent: really wicked
women are the quiet ones)   **100** *dispatch* i.e., hurry up, do it   **104** *had as
lief* would just as soon   **106–7** *if it . . . again* i.e., if my suspicions turn out
to be accurate, and I've not acted on them, can you undo my shame (Ford responds to something Page has said before they enter)   **109** *panderly* pimp-
ing; *knot* group   **110** *Now . . . shamed* i.e., now the truth will out (from the
proverb "Tell the truth and shame the devil")

113 PAGE Why, this passes! Master Ford, you are not to go
114   loose any longer; you must be pinioned.
EVANS Why, this is lunatics, this is mad as a mad dog.
SHALLOW Indeed, Master Ford, this is not well, indeed.
FORD So say I too, sir.
    [Enter Mistress Ford.]
   Come hither Mistress Ford; Mistress Ford, the honest
   woman, the modest wife; the virtuous creature that
120 hath the jealous fool to her husband! I suspect without
   cause, mistress, do I?
MRS. FORD God be my witness, you do, if you suspect
   me in any dishonesty.
124 FORD Well said, brazenface; hold it out. Come forth,
   sirrah!
    [Pulls clothes out of the basket.]
PAGE This passes!
MRS. FORD Are you not ashamed? Let the clothes alone.
FORD I shall find you anon.
EVANS 'Tis unreasonable. Will you take up your wife's
130 clothes? Come away.
FORD Empty the basket, I say!
MRS. FORD Why, man, why?
FORD Master Page, as I am a man, there was one conveyed out of my house yesterday in this basket. Why
   may not he be there again? In my house I am sure he
136 is – my intelligence is true; my jealousy is reasonable.
   Pluck me out all the linen.
138 MRS. FORD If you find a man there, he shall die a flea's
   death.
140 PAGE Here's no man.
SHALLOW By my fidelity, this is not well, Master Ford.
142   This wrongs you.

---

113 *passes* i.e., surpasses anything 114 *pinioned* tied up (a "cure" for madness) 120 *to* as 124 *hold it out* i.e., keep it up 136 *intelligence* information 138–39 *he . . . death* i.e., because he can't be any bigger than a flea
142 *wrongs* disgraces

EVANS   Master Ford, you must pray, and not follow the
imaginations of your own heart. This is jealousies.

FORD   Well, he's not here I seek for.

PAGE   No, nor nowhere else but in your brain.

FORD   Help to search my house this one time. If I find
not what I seek, show no color for my extremity – let   148
me for ever be your table sport. Let them say of me, "As   149
jealous as Ford, that searched a hollow walnut for his   150
wife's leman." Satisfy me once more; once more search   151
with me.

MRS. FORD   What ho, Mistress Page, come you and the
old woman down. My husband will come into the
chamber.

FORD   Old woman! What old woman's that?

MRS. FORD   Why, it is my maid's aunt of Brainford.

FORD   A witch, a quean, an old cozening quean! Have I   158
not forbid her my house? She comes of errands, does
she? We are simple men; we do not know what's   160
brought to pass under the profession of fortune-telling.   161
She works by charms, by spells, by the figure, and   162
such daubery as this is, beyond our element. We know   163
nothing. Come down, you witch, you hag, you; come
down, I say!

MRS. FORD   Nay, good, sweet husband! Good gentlemen,
let him not strike the old woman.

[Enter Falstaff in woman's clothes, with Mistress Page.]

MRS. PAGE   Come, Mother Prat, come, give me your   168
hand.

---

148 *show . . . extremity* i.e., make no excuse for my wild behavior   149 *table
sport* cause of mirth at dinner, laughingstock   151 *leman* lover   158 *quean*
hussy, usually a promiscuous woman; *cozening* cheating   161 *profession*
claim, pretense   162 *by the figure* (1) by making wax effigies, (2) by astro-
logical charts   163 *daubery* fakery (from "daub," to paint); *element* i.e.,
sphere of understanding   168–70 *Mother Prat . . . "prat" her* (Ford plays on
the surname: i.e., I'll smack her rear; *prat* = buttock)

170 FORD   I'll "prat" her. *[Beats him.]* Out of my door, you
171   witch, you rag, you baggage, you polecat, you runnion!
    Out, out! I'll conjure you. I'll fortune-tell you!
                                        [Falstaff runs out.]
    MRS. PAGE   Are you not ashamed? I think you have killed
    the poor woman.

    MRS. FORD   Nay, he will do it. 'Tis a goodly credit for
    you.

    FORD   Hang her, witch!

    EVANS   *[Aside]* By Jeshu, I think the 'oman is a witch in-
    deed. I like not when a 'oman has a great peard; I spy a
180   great peard under his muffler.

    FORD   Will you follow, gentlemen? I beseech you, follow.
182   See but the issue of my jealousy. If I cry out thus upon
    no trail, never trust me when I open again.

184 PAGE   Let's obey his humor a little further. Come, gentle-
    men.   *[Exeunt Ford, Page, Shallow, Caius, and Evans.]*

    MRS. PAGE   Trust me, he beat him most pitifully.

    MRS. FORD   Nay, by the mass, that he did not: he beat
    him most unpitifully, methought.

189 MRS. PAGE   I'll have the cudgel hallowed and hung o'er
190   the altar; it hath done meritorious service.

    MRS. FORD ·   What think you? May we, with the warrant
    of womanhood and the witness of a good conscience,
    pursue him with any further revenge?

    MRS. PAGE   The spirit of wantonness is, sure, scared out
195   of him. If the devil have him not in fee simple, with
196   fine and recovery, he will never, I think, in the way of
    waste, attempt us again.

---

171 *rag* worthless person; *baggage* hussy; *runnion* (another insult for a disreputable woman)   182 *issue* result   182–83 *If . . . again* i.e., if I don't find
my prey, I won't try ever again (*cry out, trail,* and *open* are hunting terms)
184 *obey* defer to   189–90 *hallowed . . . altar* i.e., like a sacred relic   195 *fee
simple* absolute possession (a legal term concerning property)   196 *fine and
recovery* (process for converting an estate to *fee simple*)   196–97 *the . . .
waste* i.e., an effort at vandalism (continuing the property metaphor)

MRS. FORD   Shall we tell our husbands how we have
served him?

MRS. PAGE   Yes, by all means, if it be but to scrape the fig-   200
ures out of your husband's brains. If they can find in
their hearts the poor unvirtuous fat knight shall be any
further afflicted, we two will still be the ministers.   203

MRS. FORD   I'll warrant they'll have him publicly
shamed, and methinks there would be no period to the   205
jest, should he not be publicly shamed.

MRS. PAGE   Come, to the forge with it; then shape it. I
would not have things cool.   *Exeunt.*

*

∾ **IV.3** *Enter Host and Bardolph.*

BARDOLPH   Sir, the German desires to have three of your   1
horses. The duke himself will be tomorrow at court,
and they are going to meet him.

HOST   What duke should that be comes so secretly? I
hear not of him in the court. Let me speak with the
gentlemen. They speak English?

BARDOLPH   Ay, sir; I'll call him to you.

HOST   They shall have my horses, but I'll make them
pay; I'll sauce them. They have had my house a week at   9
command. I have turned away my other guests. They   10
must come off; I'll sauce them. Come.   *Exeunt.*   11

*

200–1 *figures* fantasies   203 *still* ever, always; *ministers* agents, executors
205 *period* ending
    IV.3 A room in the Garter Inn   1 *German* (F is unclear about numbers;
Bardolph seems to be referring to the spokesman of the Germans, the Host
to all of them)   9 *sauce them* i.e., "soak" them, make them pay   9–10 *at
command* at their disposal   11 *come off* pay up

∾ **IV.4** *Enter Page, Ford, Mistress Page, Mistress Ford, and Evans.*

1 EVANS   'Tis one of the best discretions of a 'oman as ever I did look upon.

3 PAGE   And did he send you both these letters at an instant?

MRS. PAGE   Within a quarter of an hour.

FORD
   Pardon me, wife. Henceforth do what thou wilt:
   I rather will suspect the sun with cold
8 Than thee with wantonness. Now doth thy honor stand,
   In him that was of late an heretic,
10 As firm as faith.

PAGE   'Tis well, 'tis well; no more:
   Be not as extreme in submission as in offense.
   But let our plot go forward. Let our wives
   Yet once again, to make us public sport,
   Appoint a meeting with this old fat fellow,
   Where we may take him and disgrace him for it.

FORD
   There is no better way than that they spoke of.

PAGE   How! to send him word they'll meet him in the park at midnight? Fie, fie, he'll never come.

EVANS   You say he has been thrown in the rivers, and has
20 been grievously peaten as an old 'oman. Methinks there should be terrors in him that he should not come. Methinks his flesh is punished; he shall have no desires.

PAGE   So think I too.

MRS. FORD
   Devise but how you'll use him when he comes,
   And let us two devise to bring him thither.

IV.4 A room in the Fords' house   1 *best . . . 'oman* i.e., most discreet, sensible women   3–4 *at an instant* simultaneously   8 *honor* chastity, fidelity

MRS. PAGE

There is an old tale goes that Herne the Hunter,   26
Sometime a keeper here in Windsor Forest,   27
Doth all the wintertime, at still midnight,
Walk round about an oak, with great ragg'd horns;   29
And there he blasts the tree, and takes the cattle,   30
And makes milch kine yield blood, and shakes a chain   31
In a most hideous and dreadful manner.
You have heard of such a spirit, and well you know
The superstitious idleheaded eld   34
Received and did deliver to our age
This tale of Herne the Hunter for a truth.

PAGE

Why, yet there want not many that do fear   37
In deep of night to walk by this Herne's oak.
But what of this?

MRS. FORD   Marry, this is our device:
That Falstaff at that oak shall meet with us,   40
Disguised like Herne, with huge horns on his head.

PAGE

Well, let it not be doubted but he'll come,
And in this shape when you have brought him thither,
What shall be done with him? What is your plot?

MRS. PAGE

That likewise have we thought upon, and thus:
Nan Page my daughter, and my little son,
And three or four more of their growth, we'll dress   47
Like urchins, oafs, and fairies, green and white,   48
With rounds of waxen tapers on their heads,   49
And rattles in their hands. Upon a sudden,   50
As Falstaff, she, and I are newly met,

---

26 *Herne the Hunter* (the legend is apparently Shakespeare's invention) 27
Sometime formerly; *a keeper* an officer in charge of the forest grounds 29
ragg'd irregular, jagged 30 *blasts* blights; *takes* bewitches 31 *milch kine*
dairy cattle 34 *idleheaded eld* ignorant people of former ages 37 *yet* even
now; *want not* are not lacking 47 *growth* size 48 *urchins, oafs* elves, children of elves 49 *tapers* candles

52   Let them from forth a saw pit rush at once
53   With some diffusèd song. Upon their sight,
54   We two in great amazedness will fly.
     Then let them all encircle him about,
56   And, fairylike, to pinch the unclean knight,
     And ask him why, that hour of fairy revel,
     In their so sacred paths he dares to tread
     In shape profane.

MRS. FORD   And till he tell the truth,
60   Let the supposèd fairies pinch him sound
     And burn him with their tapers.

MRS. PAGE   The truth being known,
     We'll all present ourselves, dis-horn the spirit,
     And mock him home to Windsor.

FORD   The children must
     Be practiced well to this, or they'll ne'er do't.

EVANS   I will teach the children their behaviors; and I
66   will be like a jackanapes also, to burn the knight with
     my taber.

FORD
68   That will be excellent. I'll go buy them vizards.

MRS. PAGE
     My Nan shall be the queen of all the fairies,
70   Finely attirèd in a robe of white.

PAGE
     That silk will I go buy. *[Aside]* And in that time
     Shall Master Slender steal my Nan away,
73   And marry her at Eton. – Go, send to Falstaff straight.

FORD
     Nay, I'll to him again in name of Brook.
     He'll tell me all his purpose. Sure, he'll come.

---

52 *saw pit* large hole in the ground (timber to be sawed was placed across it) 53 *diffusèd* wild, confused   54 *amazedness* terror, bewilderment   56 *unclean* immoral, lustful   60 *sound* soundly (i.e., hard)   66 *be . . . jackanapes* i.e., behave like a monkey   68 *vizards* masks   73 *Eton* a village across the Thames from Windsor; *straight* straightaway, quickly

MRS. PAGE
  Fear not you that. Go, get us properties   76
  And tricking for our fairies.   77
EVANS   Let us about it. It is admirable pleasures and fery
  honest knaveries.   *[Exeunt Page, Ford, and Evans.]*
MRS. PAGE
  Go, Mistress Ford,   80
  Send Quickly to Sir John, to know his mind.
                         [Exit Mistress Ford.]
  I'll to the doctor: he hath my good will,
  And none but he, to marry with Nan Page.
  That Slender, though well landed, is an idiot;
  And he my husband best of all affects.   85
  The doctor is well moneyed, and his friends
  Potent at court. He, none but he, shall have her,
  Though twenty thousand worthier come to crave her.
                             [Exit.]

∾ IV.5 *Enter Host, [and] Simple.*

HOST   What wouldst thou have, boor? What, thickskin?
  Speak, breathe, discuss; brief, short, quick, snap.
SIMPLE   Marry, sir, I come to speak with Sir John Falstaff
  from Master Slender.
HOST   There's his chamber, his house, his castle, his
  standing bed and truckle bed. 'Tis painted about with 6
  the story of the Prodigal, fresh and new. Go, knock and 7
  call. He'll speak like an anthropophaginian unto thee. 8
  Knock, I say.
SIMPLE   There's an old woman, a fat woman, gone up 10
  into his chamber. I'll be so bold as stay, sir, till she come
  down. I come to speak with her, indeed.

---

76 *properties* i.e., stage props 77 *tricking* adornment, finery 85 *affects*
likes, approves
    IV.5 A room in the Garter Inn 6 *truckle bed* trundle bed stored under
the *standing bed* 7 *story of the Prodigal* (biblical parable of the wicked son
who wastes his fortune in lust, lives with swine, and finally repents; see Luke
15) 8 *an anthropophaginian* a cannibal

HOST   Ha, a fat woman? The knight may be robbed: I'll
14   call. Bully knight, bully Sir John! Speak from thy lungs
15   military: art thou there? It is thine host, thine Ephesian,
calls.

FALSTAFF   *[Above]* How now, mine host?

18   HOST   Here's a Bohemian-Tartar tarries the coming
down of thy fat woman. Let her descend, bully, let her
20   descend. My chambers are honorable. Fie, privacy, fie!
[Enter] Falstaff.

FALSTAFF   There was, mine host, an old fat woman even
now with me, but she's gone.

SIMPLE   Pray you, sir, was't not the wise woman of Brainford?

25   FALSTAFF   Ay, marry, was it, mussel shell. What would
you with her?

SIMPLE   My master, sir, my Master Slender, sent to her,
28   seeing her go through the streets, to know, sir, whether
29   one Nym, sir, that beguiled him of a chain, had the
30   chain or no.

FALSTAFF   I spake with the old woman about it.

SIMPLE   And what says she, I pray, sir?

FALSTAFF   Marry, she says that the very same man that
beguiled Master Slender of his chain cozened him of it.

SIMPLE   I would I could have spoken with the woman
herself. I had other things to have spoken with her too,
from him.

FALSTAFF   What are they? let us know.

HOST   Ay, come; quick.

40   SIMPLE   I may not conceal them, sir.

14–15 *lungs military* (this inversion is another of the Host's pretentious figures of speech)   **15** *Ephesian* i.e., the Host's term for "companion" (possibly
connoting loose living: see Paul's caution in his "Epistle to the Ephesians,"
4:22)   **18** *Bohemian-Tartar* i.e., barbarian (referring to Simple)   **20** *privacy*
concealment   **25** *mussel shell* i.e., one who (1) gapes, (2) is empty-headed
28–30 *to know . . . or no* (Slender seems to be privately consulting a fortune-
teller about his stolen property [see I.1.140–57] and about his marriage
prospects)   **29** *beguiled* cheated, cozened (setting up the joke in ll. 33–34)
40 *conceal* (error for "reveal")

HOST   Conceal them, or thou diest.

SIMPLE   Why, sir, they were nothing but about Mistress
Anne Page; to know if it were my master's fortune to
have her, or no.

FALSTAFF   'Tis, 'tis his fortune.

SIMPLE   What, sir?

FALSTAFF   To have her, or no. Go, say the woman told
me so.

SIMPLE   May I be bold to say so, sir?

FALSTAFF   Ay, Sir Tyke; who more bold?   50

SIMPLE   I thank your worship: I shall make my master
glad with these tidings.   *[Exit.]*

HOST   Thou art clerkly, thou art clerkly, Sir John. Was 53
there a wise woman with thee?

FALSTAFF   Ay, that there was, mine host: one that hath
taught me more wit than ever I learned before in my   56
life; and I paid nothing for it neither, but was paid for
my learning.

[Enter] Bardolph.

BARDOLPH   Out, alas, sir, cozenage, mere cozenage!   59

HOST   Where be my horses? Speak well of them, varletto. 60

BARDOLPH   Run away, with the cozeners; for so soon as I
came beyond Eton, they threw me off from behind one
of them, in a slough of mire; and set spurs and away,   63
like three German devils, three Doctor Faustasses.   64

HOST   They are gone but to meet the duke, villain. Do   65
not say they be fled: Germans are honest men.

[Enter] Evans.

EVANS   Where is mine host?

HOST   What is the matter, sir?

---

50 *Tyke* mongrel   53 *clerkly* wise, scholarly   56 *wit* wisdom   59 *mere cozenage* total trickery   60 *varletto* varlet, rascal   63 *slough of mire* swampy bog
64 *Doctor Faustasses* (reference to Marlowe's *Tragedy of Doctor Faustus,* c.
1592, in which the scholar-hero sells his soul to the devil; with pun on
"asses")   65 *duke* (perhaps a reference to the German Duke of Würtemberg,
a candidate for the Order of the Garter: see below, l. 80, and Introduction,
pp. xxxiv–xxxv); *villain* rascal

EVANS   Have a care of your entertainments. There is a
70   friend of mine come to town, tells me there is three
71   Cozen-Garmombles that has cozened all the hosts of
72   Readings, of Maidenhead, of Colebrook, of horses and
     money. I tell you for good will, look you: you are wise
     and full of gibes and vloutingstocks, and 'tis not conve-
     nient you should be cozened. Fare you well.   *[Exit.]*
     [Enter] Caius.

CAIUS   Vere is mine host de Jarteer?

HOST   Here, Master Doctor, in perplexity and doubtful
     dilemma.

CAIUS   I cannot tell vat is dat; but it is tell-a me dat you
80   make grand preparation for a duke de Jamany. By my
     trot, dere is no duke that the court is know to come. I
     tell you for good will; adieu.   *[Exit.]*
83   HOST   Hue and cry, villain, go! Assist me, knight! I am
     undone! Fly, run, hue and cry, villain! I am undone!
     [Exeunt Host and Bardolph.]

FALSTAFF   I would all the world might be cozened, for I
     have been cozened and beaten too. If it should come to
     the ear of the court how I have been transformed, and
     how my transformation hath been washed and cud-
     geled, they would melt me out of my fat drop by drop,
90   and liquor fishermen's boots with me. I warrant they
91   would whip me with their fine wits till I were as crest-
92   fallen as a dried pear. I never prospered since I forswore
93   myself at primero. Well, if my wind were but long
     enough, I would repent.
     [Enter Mistress] Quickly.
     Now, whence come you?

---

71 *Cozen-Garmombles* (1) perhaps Evans's pronunciation of "Cozen-German nobles" – i.e., cousin Germans, near relatives, (2) cheating Germans   72 *Readings . . . Maidenhead . . . Colebrook* towns in the Thames valley near Windsor   83 *Hue and cry* (the familiar shout for chasing a criminal)   90 *liquor* grease (i.e., waterproof)   91–92 *crestfallen* shriveled   92–93 *forswore . . . primero* cheated at the popular card game primero and then denied it   93 *wind* breath

QUICKLY   From the two parties forsooth.

FALSTAFF   The devil take one party and his dam the   97
other! — and so they shall be both bestowed. I have suffered more for their sakes, more than the villainous in-
constancy of man's disposition is able to bear.   *100*

QUICKLY   And have not they suffered? Yes, I warrant;
speciously one of them. Mistress Ford, good heart, is
beaten black and blue, that you cannot see a white spot
about her.

FALSTAFF   What tell'st thou me of black and blue? I was
beaten myself into all the colors of the rainbow; and I
was like to be apprehended for the witch of Brainford.
But that my admirable dexterity of wit, my counterfeit-
ing the action of an old woman, delivered me, the
knave constable had set me i' the stocks, i' the common   *110*
stocks, for a witch.

QUICKLY   Sir, let me speak with you in your chamber.
You shall hear how things go, and, I warrant, to your
content. Here is a letter will say somewhat. Good
hearts, what ado here is to bring you together. Sure,
one of you does not serve heaven well, that you are so
crossed.   117

FALSTAFF   Come up into my chamber.   *Exeunt.*

*

∾ **IV.6** *Enter Fenton, [and] Host.*

HOST   Master Fenton, talk not to me. My mind is heavy;
I will give over all.   2

FENTON
Yet hear me speak. Assist me in my purpose,
And, as I am a gentleman, I'll give thee

---

97 *his dam* his mother (from a proverbial phrase, "the devil and his dam")
117 *crossed* thwarted, unfortunate (as in "star-crossed")
    IV.6 A room in the Garter Inn   **2** *give over all* i.e., suspend my efforts on
your behalf

A hundred pound in gold more than your loss.

HOST   I will hear you, Master Fenton, and I will, at the
least, keep your counsel.

FENTON

From time to time I have acquainted you
With the dear love I bear to fair Anne Page,
10 Who mutually hath answered my affection,
So far forth as herself might be her chooser,
Even to my wish. I have a letter from her
Of such contents as you will wonder at,
14 The mirth whereof so larded with my matter
15 That neither singly can be manifested
Without the show of both. Fat Falstaff
17 Hath a great scene. The image of the jest
18 I'll show you here at large.
    [Shows a letter.]   Hark, good mine host:
Tonight at Herne's Oak, just twixt twelve and one,
20 Must my sweet Nan present the Fairy Queen –
The purpose why, is here – in which disguise,
22 While other jests are something rank on foot,
Her father hath commanded her to slip
Away with Slender, and with him at Eton
Immediately to marry. She hath consented. Now sir,
26 Her mother (even strong against that match
And firm for Doctor Caius) hath appointed
28 That he shall likewise shuffle her away,
29 While other sports are tasking of their minds,
30 And at the deanery, where a priest attends,
Straight marry her. To this her mother's plot
She, seemingly obedient, likewise hath

---

14 *larded* intermixed; *my matter* what concerns me 15–16 *neither . . . both*
i.e., the plots to humiliate Falstaff and to marry secretly are completely inter-
dependent 17 *great scene* major role; *image* outline, form 18 *at large* in detail 20 *present* impersonate, take the role of 22 *something rank* very
abundantly 26 *even* equally, just as 28 *shuffle* smuggle (hurriedly) 29
tasking of occupying 30 *deanery* home of the priest serving as dean of the
chapel (perhaps specifically Saint George's Chapel within the walls of Windsor Castle)

Made promise to the doctor. Now, thus it rests:
Her father means she shall be all in white,
And in that habit, when Slender sees his time   35
To take her by the hand and bid her go,
She shall go with him. Her mother hath intended,
The better to denote her to the doctor   38
(For they must all be masked and vizarded),
That quaint in green she shall be loose enrobed,   40
With ribbons pendent, flaring 'bout her head;
And when the doctor spies his vantage ripe,
To pinch her by the hand, and on that token
The maid hath given consent to go with him.

HOST
Which means she to deceive, father or mother?

FENTON
Both, my good host, to go along with me.
And here it rests, that you'll procure the vicar   47
To stay for me at church twixt twelve and one,
And, in the lawful name of marrying,
To give our hearts united ceremony.   50

HOST
Well, husband your device; I'll to the vicar.   51
Bring you the maid, you shall not lack a priest.

FENTON
So shall I evermore be bound to thee;
Besides, I'll make a present recompense.   *Exeunt.* 54

*

∾ **V.1** *Enter Falstaff, [and Mistress] Quickly.*

FALSTAFF Prithee no more prattling. Go: I'll hold. This   1
is the third time; I hope good luck lies in odd numbers.

---

35 *habit* costume 38 *denote* indicate 40 *quaint* elaborately 47 *rests*
stands 50 *united ceremony* the ritual of union in marriage 51 *husband*
manage carefully (with a characteristic play on the familiar noun) 54 *a present* an immediate
V.1 A room in the Garter Inn 1 *hold* keep my promise

3 Away; go. They say there is divinity in odd numbers, ei-
4 ther in nativity, chance, or death. Away.

QUICKLY   I'll provide you a chain, and I'll do what I can
to get you a pair of horns.

7 FALSTAFF   Away, I say; time wears. Hold up your head,
8 and mince.   *[Exit Mistress Quickly.]*
       [Enter] Ford.

   How now, Master Brook? Master Brook, the matter
10 will be known tonight, or never. Be you in the park
   about midnight, at Herne's Oak, and you shall see
   wonders.

13 FORD   Went you not to her yesterday, sir, as you told me
   you had appointed?

FALSTAFF   I went to her, Master Brook, as you see, like a
   poor old man, but I came from her, Master Brook, like
   a poor old woman. That same knave Ford, her husband, hath the finest mad devil of jealousy in him,
19 Master Brook, that ever governed frenzy. I will tell you:
20 he beat me grievously, in the shape of a woman; for in
21 the shape of man, Master Brook, I fear not Goliath
22 with a weaver's beam, because I know also life is a shuttle. I am in haste. Go along with me; I'll tell you all,
24 Master Brook. Since I plucked geese, played truant,
   and whipped top, I knew not what 'twas to be beaten
   till lately. Follow me. I'll tell you strange things of this
   knave Ford, on whom tonight I will be revenged, and I
   will deliver his wife into your hand. Follow. Strange
   things in hand, Master Brook! Follow.   *Exeunt.*

                              *

---

3 *divinity* divine power 4 *nativity . . . death* i.e., it is good luck on an odd-
numbered day to be born, to undertake a venture, or to die 7 *wears* moves
along, runs out 8 *mince* i.e., run along, in that affected way you walk 13
yesterday (one of the confusions of time in the play: Falstaff's escape as the
old woman has occurred earlier in the present dramatic day) 19 *governed
frenzy* caused madness 21–22 *Goliath . . . beam* (Goliath is a biblical giant
defeated by David: his "spear was like a weaver's beam," 1 Samuel 17:7)
22–23 *shuttle* (another weaver's tool: a biblical image of the brevity of life,
Job 7:6) 24–25 *plucked . . . top* (childish activities; a top was spun with a
kind of whip)

∾ **V.2** *Enter Page, Shallow, [and] Slender.*

PAGE Come, come; we'll couch i' the castle ditch till we 1
  see the light of our fairies. Remember, son Slender, my –
SLENDER Ay, forsooth; I have spoke with her and we
  have a nayword how to know one another. I come to 4
  her in white, and cry "mum"; she cries "budget"; and 5
  by that we know one another.
SHALLOW That's good too. But what needs either your
  "mum," or her "budget"? The white will decipher her 8
  well enough. It hath struck ten o'clock.
PAGE The night is dark; light and spirits will become it 10
  well. Heaven prosper our sport. No man means evil but
  the devil, and we shall know him by his horns. Let's
  away; follow me.   *Exeunt.*

                        *

∾ **V.3** *Enter Mistress Page, Mistress Ford, [and Doctor]*
  Caius.

MRS. PAGE Master Doctor, my daughter is in green.
  When you see your time, take her by the hand, away
  with her to the deanery, and dispatch it quickly. Go be- 3
  fore into the park. We two must go together.
CAIUS I know vat I have to do. Adieu.
MRS. PAGE Fare you well, sir. *[Exit Caius.]* My husband
  will not rejoice so much at the abuse of Falstaff, as he
  will chafe at the doctor's marrying my daughter. But 'tis 8
  no matter: better a little chiding than a great deal of 9
  heartbreak.   10
MRS. FORD Where is Nan now, and her troop of fairies,
  and the Welsh devil, Hugh?

V.2 Windsor Park 1 *couch* lie hidden 4 *nayword* signal, password
5 *mum . . . budget* ("mumbudget" is believed to be a term from a children's
game indicating silence) 8 *decipher* distinguish, reveal
    V.3 The park 3 *dispatch it* i.e., get the marriage over with 8 *chafe at*
be sore about (i.e., resist) 9 *chiding* quarreling

MRS. PAGE   They are all couched in a pit hard by Herne's
Oak, with obscured lights, which at the very instant of
Falstaff's and our meeting they will at once display to
the night.

MRS. FORD   That cannot choose but amaze him.

MRS. PAGE   If he be not amazed, he will be mocked; if he
be amazed, he will every way be mocked.

20 MRS. FORD   We'll betray him finely.

MRS. PAGE

21   Against such lewdsters and their lechery,
Those that betray them do no treachery.

MRS. FORD   The hour draws on. To the oak, to the oak!

> *Exeunt.*

*

∾ **V.4** *Enter Evans [as a Satyr] and [others as] Fairies.*

1 EVANS   Trib, trib, fairies. Come, and remember your
parts. Be pold, I pray you. Follow me into the pit, and
when I give the watch'ords, do as I pid you. Come,
come. Trib, trib!   *Exeunt.*

*

∾ **V.5** *Enter Falstaff [disguised as Herne, wearing a
buck's head].*

FALSTAFF   The Windsor bell hath struck twelve; the
minute draws on. Now, the hot-blooded gods assist me!

3   Remember, Jove, thou wast a bull for thy Europa: love
set on thy horns. O powerful love, that in some respects
makes a beast a man; in some other, a man a beast. You
were also, Jupiter, a swan for the love of Leda. O om-

7   nipotent love, how near the god drew to the complex-

---

21 *lewdsters* lewd people
  V.4 Windsor Park   1 *Trib* i.e., trip, come along
  V.5 The park   3–6 *Remember . . . Leda* (Falstaff recalls the sexual exploits
of *Jove* (the Roman *Jupiter*), who took the shape of a *bull* to abduct *Europa*,
and that of a *swan* to rape *Leda*)   7–8 *complexion* nature, makeup

ion of a goose! A fault done first in the form of a beast –
O Jove, a beastly fault! – and then another fault in the
semblance of a fowl. Think on't, Jove; a foul fault! 10
When gods have hot backs, what shall poor men do? 11
For me, I am here a Windsor stag; and the fattest, I
think, i' th' forest. Send me a cool rut time, Jove, or 13
who can blame me to piss my tallow? Who comes here? 14
my doe?

[Enter] Mistress Page, [and] Mistress Ford.

MRS. FORD   Sir John? Art thou there, my deer, my male
deer?

FALSTAFF   My doe with the black scut! Let the sky rain 18
potatoes; let it thunder to the tune of "Greensleeves," 19
hail kissing comfits, and snow eryngoes. Let there come 20
a tempest of provocation, I will shelter me here. 21

[Embraces her.]

MRS. FORD   Mistress Page is come with me, sweetheart.

FALSTAFF   Divide me like a bribed buck, each a haunch. I 23
will keep my sides to myself, my shoulders for the fel- 24
low of this walk, and my horns I bequeath your hus- 25
bands. Am I a woodman, ha? Speak I like Herne the 26
Hunter? Why, now is Cupid a child of conscience; he 27
makes restitution. As I am a true spirit, welcome! 28

[Noise within.]

MRS. PAGE   Alas, what noise?

MRS. FORD   Heaven forgive our sins! 30

---

10 *foul fault* (the similar pronunciation of these words probably emphasized
the play on *foul* and *fowl*)   11 *hot backs* i.e., powerful lusts (a strong back
was a metonymy for male sexual talent)   13 *rut time* mating season   14 *piss
my tallow* urinate all my fat (bucks at mating season grow lean)   18 *scut* tail
of a deer (with the sexual sense of "tail")   19 *potatoes* i.e., sweet potatoes
(thought to be an aphrodisiac)   20 *kissing comfits* candies used to sweeten
the breath; *eryngoes* candied roots of the sea holly (also supposed an aphrodisiac)   21 *provocation* i.e., other sexual temptations   23 *bribed* stolen   24–
25 *fellow . . . walk* i.e., keeper   25–26 *horns . . . husbands* i.e., by cuckolding
them   26 *woodman* (1) hunter, (2) hunter of women, roué   27–28
Cupid . . . restitution i.e., Cupid must have developed a conscience because
he makes up for my earlier humiliations   28 *true spirit* i.e., reincarnation of
Herne the Hunter

FALSTAFF   What should this be?

MRS. FORD, MRS. PAGE   Away, away!   *[They run off.]*

33 FALSTAFF   I think the devil will not have me damned lest
the oil that's in me should set hell on fire. He would
never else cross me thus.

*Enter Evans [as a Satyr, Mistress] Quickly, Anne Page,
[and others as] Fairies, [with tapers, and] Pistol [as
Hobgoblin].*

QUICKLY

Fairies, black, gray, green, and white,

You moonshine revelers, and shades of night,

38   You orphan heirs of fixèd destiny,

39   Attend your office and your quality.

40   Crier Hobgoblin, make the fairy oyes.

PISTOL

41   Elves, list your names; silence, you airy toys!

42   Cricket, to Windsor chimneys shalt thou leap.

Where fires thou find'st unraked and hearths unswept,

44   There pinch the maids as blue as bilberry.

45   Our radiant queen hates sluts and sluttery.

FALSTAFF

46   They are fairies; he that speaks to them shall die.

47   I'll wink and couch; no man their works must eye.

[Lies facedown on the ground.]

EVANS

48   Where's Bead? Go you, and where you find a maid

That ere she sleep has thrice her prayers said,

33–35 *I think . . . thus* i.e., Satan won't permit me to sin, fearing my com-
bustible fat, and so keeps thwarting me   38 *orphan* (fairies had no fathers);
heirs . . . destiny (fairies traditionally performed [inherited] certain supernatural or unseen tasks)   39 *Attend . . . quality* i.e., do your jobs and fulfill your
roles   40 *Crier Hobgoblin* i.e., Robin Goodfellow or Puck, the fairies' town
crier; *oyes* (from the French word *oyez,* meaning "hark ye," pronounced to
rhyme with *toys* in the next line)   41 *list* listen for; *airy toys* insubstantial
spirits   42 *Cricket* (nickname for fairy assigned to *chimneys* and *hearths*)   44
bilberry (a kind of blueberry)   45 *radiant queen* Queen of the Fairies (but
with a glance at Elizabeth I); *sluttery* disorder and squalor (both physical and
moral)   46 *he . . . die* (an old superstition)   47 *wink and couch* i.e., close my
eyes and hide   48 *Bead* (fairy name, denoting small size)

Raise up the organs of her fantasy,   50
Sleep she as sound as careless infancy.
But those as sleep and think not on their sins,
Pinch them – arms, legs, backs, shoulders, sides, and shins.
QUICKLY
About, about:
Search Windsor Castle, elves, within and out.
Strew good luck, oafs, on every sacred room,
That it may stand till the perpetual doom,   57
In state as wholesome as in state 'tis fit,   58
Worthy the owner, and the owner it.
The several chairs of order look you scour   60
With juice of balm and every precious flower.   61
Each fair installment, coat, and sev'ral crest,   62
With loyal blazon, evermore be blessed.   63
And nightly, meadow fairies, look you sing,
Like to the Garter's compass, in a ring.   65
Th' expressure that it bears, green let it be,   66
More fertile-fresh than all the field to see;
And *Honi soit qui mal y pense* write   68
In em'rald tufts, flow'rs purple, blue, and white,   69
Like sapphire, pearl, and rich embroidery,   70
Buckled below fair knighthood's bending knee –
Fairies use flow'rs for their charactery.   72
Away, disperse. But till 'tis one o'clock,

---

50 *Raise . . . fantasy* i.e., elevate her imagination, to produce sweet dreams 57 *perpetual doom* Judgment Day (the Judeo-Christian belief that the world will end with God's judgment, or doom, of mankind) 58 *state as wholesome . . . fit* i.e., a solid condition (*state*) appropriate to its important status 60 *chairs of order* seats (stalls) of the Garter knights in the choir of the Windsor chapel 61 *balm* fragrant herb 62 *installment* stall, seat; *coat . . . crest* heraldic decorations painted on the stalls 63 *loyal blazon* heroic banner hanging above the stall 65 *Garter's compass* i.e., a circle (the emblem of the Order of the Garter is a blue circular ribbon worn below the knee) 66 *expressure . . . bears* i.e., the appearance of the pressed circle on the grass (the "fairy ring") 68 *Honi soit qui mal y pense* Shame to him who thinks evil (the motto of the Order of the Garter: according to legend, King Edward III spoke the phrase to tittering courtiers when he picked up a lady's garter from the floor; *pense* is pronounced with two syllables) 69 *tufts* bunches 72 *charactery* writing (pronounced "ka-rák-ter-y")

Our dance of custom round about the oak
Of Herne the Hunter, let us not forget.

EVANS

Pray you, lock hand in hand; yourselves in order set;
And twenty glowworms shall our lanterns be,

78   To guide our measure round about the tree.

79   But, stay! I smell a man of middle earth.

80   FALSTAFF   Heavens defend me from that Welsh fairy, lest
he transform me to a piece of cheese!

PISTOL

82   Vile worm, thou wast o'erlooked even in thy birth.

QUICKLY

With trial fire touch me his finger end.
If he be chaste, the flame will back descend

85   And turn him to no pain; but if he start,
It is the flesh of a corrupted heart.

PISTOL

A trial, come.

EVANS   Come, will this wood take fire?
    [They burn him with their tapers.]

FALSTAFF   O, O, O!

QUICKLY

Corrupt, corrupt and tainted in desire!

90   About him, fairies, sing a scornful rhyme;

91   And, as you trip, still pinch him to your time.

The Song.

Fie on sinful fantasy!

93   Fie on lust and luxury!

94   Lust is but a bloody fire,
Kindled with unchaste desire,
Fed in heart, whose flames aspire,
As thoughts do blow them, higher and higher.

---

78 *measure* dance   79 *middle earth* the realm of mortals, between heaven and hell   80–81 *Heavens . . . cheese* (another reference to the Welsh fondness for cheese)   82 *o'erlooked* bewitched, watched over (with the evil eye)   85 *start* jump or flinch (as in "startle")   91 *to your time* i.e., in rhythm   93 *luxury* sensuality   94 *a bloody fire* i.e., passionate burning in the blood

Pinch him, fairies, mutually;   98
Pinch him for his villainy;
Pinch him, and burn him, and turn him about,   100
Till candles and starlight and moonshine be out.

[During this song they pinch Falstaff. Doctor] Caius
[comes one way and steals away a Fairy in green],
Slender [another way and takes off a Fairy in white,
and] Fenton [comes and steals away Anne Page.
A noise of hunting is heard within. All the Fairies run
away. Falstaff rises].
[Enter] Page, Ford [, Mistress Page, and Mistress Ford].

PAGE
Nay, do not fly: I think we have watched you now.   102
Will none but Herne the Hunter serve your turn?

MRS. PAGE
I pray you, come, hold up the jest no higher.   104
Now, good Sir John, how like you Windsor wives?
See you these, husband? Do not these fair yokes   106
Become the forest better than the town?   107

FORD   Now sir, who's a cuckold now? Master Brook, Fal- 108
staff's a knave, a cuckoldy knave; here are his horns,
Master Brook. And, Master Brook, he hath enjoyed   110
nothing of Ford's but his buck basket, his cudgel, and
twenty pounds of money, which must be paid to Master Brook; his horses are arrested for it, Master Brook.   113

MRS. FORD   Sir John, we have had ill luck; we could
never meet. I will never take you for my love again, but 115
I will always count you my deer.

FALSTAFF   I do begin to perceive that I am made an ass.

FORD   Ay, and an ox too: both the proofs are extant.   118

---

98 *mutually* in unison   **102** *watched you* spied on you, caught you in the act
(Page's feigned anger is addressed to Mrs. Page)   **104** *hold . . . higher* i.e.,
let's prolong the charade no further   **106** *yokes* antlers (i.e., Falstaff's horns)
107 *Become* suit   **108–13** *Master Brook . . . Brook* (throughout this speech
Ford mimics Falstaff's repetitive use of the name in their earlier conversations)   **113** *arrested for it* seized as collateral   **115** *meet* i.e., to make love
118 *both . . . extant* i.e., two pieces of evidence are present (Falstaff is an *ass*
because he has been fooled and an *ox* because he is wearing horns)

FALSTAFF   And these are not fairies? I was three or four
times in the thought they were not fairies; and yet the
guiltiness of my mind, the sudden surprise of my powers, drove the grossness of the foppery into a received
belief, in despite of the teeth of all rhyme and reason,
that they were fairies. See now how wit may be made a
Jack-a-Lent, when 'tis upon ill employment.

EVANS   Sir John Falstaff, serve Got and leave your desires, and fairies will not pinse you.

FORD   Well said, fairy Hugh.

EVANS   And leave you your jealousies too, I pray you.

FORD   I will never mistrust my wife again, till thou art
able to woo her in good English.

FALSTAFF   Have I laid my brain in the sun and dried it,
that it wants matter to prevent so gross o'erreaching as
this? Am I ridden with a Welsh goat too? Shall I have a
coxcomb of frieze? 'Tis time I were choked with a piece
of toasted cheese.

EVANS   Seese is not good to give putter – your belly is all
putter.

FALSTAFF   "Seese" and "putter"! Have I lived to stand at
the taunt of one that makes fritters of English? This
is enough to be the decay of lust and late walking
through the realm.

MRS. PAGE   Why, Sir John, do you think, though we
would have thrust virtue out of our hearts by the head

121–22 *surprise . . . powers* ambush of my wits   122–24 *drove . . . fairies* i.e.,
made me, against common sense, accept their absurd disguises (*foppery*) as
genuine   125 *Jack-a-Lent* i.e., puppet abused in a carnival game (as at
III.3.22)   133 *wants matter* i.e., lacks the good sense   134 *ridden with*
tricked by, taken advantage of; *Welsh goat* (the quarto text casts Evans in the
charade "like a Satyre," half man and half goat, perhaps represented by a
horned mask; or, since Wales was famous for its flocks, *goat* may be another
nationalist insult suggesting stupidity or lust)   135 *coxcomb of frieze* fool's
cap made of coarse Welsh cloth   137 *give* add to   140 *makes fritters of* chops
up, batters, and fries   141 *decay . . . late walking* i.e., the end of whoring
and other nocturnal mischief   143–46 *though we . . . hell* i.e., even if we had
decided to be wicked

and shoulders, and have given ourselves without scruple to hell, that ever the devil could have made you our delight?

FORD　What, a hodge-pudding? a bag of flax?　148

MRS. PAGE　A puffed man?

PAGE　Old, cold, withered, and of intolerable entrails?　150

FORD　And one that is as slanderous as Satan?　151

PAGE　And as poor as Job?

FORD　And as wicked as his wife?　153

EVANS　And given to fornications, and to taverns, and sack and wine and metheglins, and to drinkings and　155 swearings and starings, pribbles and prabbles?

FALSTAFF　Well, I am your theme. You have the start of　157 me; I am dejected; I am not able to answer the Welsh　158 flannel. Ignorance itself is a plummet o'er me; use me as　159 you will.　*160*

FORD　Marry, sir, we'll bring you to Windsor, to one Master Brook, that you have cozened of money, to whom you should have been a pander. Over and above　163 that you have suffered, I think to repay that money will be a biting affliction.

PAGE　Yet be cheerful, knight. Thou shalt eat a posset　166 tonight at my house, where I will desire thee to laugh at my wife that now laughs at thee. Tell her, Master Slender hath married her daughter.

MRS. PAGE　*[Aside]* Doctors doubt that. If Anne Page be　170 my daughter, she is, by this, Doctor Caius' wife.　171

　[Enter Slender.]

---

148 *hodge-pudding* sausage stuffed with a mixture of ingredients; *bag of flax* i.e., a bulky sack　150 *intolerable entrails* unbearably large guts　151 *slanderous* prone to lying　153 *wife* (Job's wife was a familiar emblem for blasphemy; see Job 2:9)　155 *metheglins* Welsh spiced mead　157 *start of* better of (common phrase from racing)　158 *dejected* brought low, humiliated　159 *flannel* (another Welsh cloth); *is . . . me* i.e., has not sunk as low as I have (with a play on *plummet* / "plumbet," another woolen cloth)　163 *pander* pimp　166 *eat a posset* enjoy a hot, spiced drink　170 *Doctors doubt that* scholars disagree (proverbial phrase of disbelief, alluding here to her scheme with Doctor Caius)　171 *by this* i.e., by this time, by now

SLENDER Whoa, ho, ho, father Page!

173 PAGE Son, how now; how now, son? Have you dispatched?

175 SLENDER Dispatched? I'll make the best in Gloucestershire know on't; would I were hanged, la, else.

PAGE Of what, son?

SLENDER I came yonder at Eton to marry Mistress Anne
179 Page, and she's a great lubberly boy. If it had not been i'
180 the church, I would have swinged him, or he should have swinged me. If I did not think it had been Anne
182 Page, would I might never stir – and 'tis a postmaster's boy.

PAGE Upon my life, then, you took the wrong.

SLENDER What need you tell me that? I think so, when I
186 took a boy for a girl. If I had been married to him, for
187 all he was in woman's apparel, I would not have had him.

PAGE Why, this is your own folly. Did not I tell you how
190 you should know my daughter by her garments?

SLENDER I went to her in white, and cried "mum," and she cried "budget," as Anne and I had appointed; and yet it was not Anne, but a postmaster's boy.

MRS. PAGE Good George, be not angry. I knew of your
195 purpose, turned my daughter into green, and indeed she is now with the doctor at the deanery, and there married.

[Enter Doctor Caius.]

CAIUS Vere is Mistress Page? By gar, I am cozened – I ha'
199 married *un garçon,* a boy; *un paysan,* by gar. A boy, it is
200 not Anne Page. By gar, I am cozened.

MRS. PAGE Why, did you take her in green?

173–74 *dispatched* succeeded, finished the job 175 *best* gentry, the "important people" 179 *great lubberly* large and clumsy 180 *swinged* beaten (rhymes with "hinged") 182–83 *postmaster's boy* stableboy who served the master of the post horses 186 *took* mistook 186–87 *for all* even though 187–88 *had him* i.e., (1) kept him as my wife, (2) had sex with him, consummated the "marriage" 195 *turned my daughter* i.e., changed her costume 199 *un paysan* a peasant (boy)

CAIUS   Ay, by gar, and 'tis a boy. By gar, I'll raise all   202
Windsor.   *[Exit.]*

FORD   This is strange. Who hath got the right Anne?

PAGE   My heart misgives me. Here comes Master Fen-   205
ton.

[Enter Fenton and Anne Page.]
How now, Master Fenton?

ANNE
Pardon, good father; good my mother, pardon.

PAGE   Now, mistress, how chance you went not with
Master Slender?   210

MRS. PAGE
Why went you not with Master Doctor, maid?

FENTON
You do amaze her. Hear the truth of it.   212
You would have married her most shamefully,
Where there was no proportion held in love.   214
The truth is, she and I, long since contracted,   215
Are now so sure that nothing can dissolve us.   216
Th' offense is holy that she hath committed,
And this deceit loses the name of craft,
Of disobedience, or unduteous title,   219
Since therein she doth evitate and shun   220
A thousand irreligious cursèd hours,
Which forcèd marriage would have brought upon her.

FORD
Stand not amazed. Here is no remedy.
In love the heavens themselves do guide the state;
Money buys lands, and wives are sold by fate.

FALSTAFF   I am glad, though you have ta'en a special
stand to strike at me, that your arrow hath glanced.   227

PAGE
Well, what remedy? Fenton, heaven give thee joy!

---

202 *raise* arouse to arms   205 *misgives* warns, troubles   212 *amaze* bewilder,
overwhelm   214 *proportion held* i.e., equality or mutuality between the two
people   215 *contracted* engaged   216 *sure* secure, safe   219 *unduteous title*
i.e., being called undutiful   220 *evitate* avoid   227 *stand* place for shooting
(i.e., a deer stand); *glanced* struck indirectly (i.e., gone awry)

229 . What cannot be eschewed must be embraced.

FALSTAFF

230 When night dogs run, all sorts of deer are chased.

MRS. PAGE

231 Well, I will muse no further. Master Fenton,
Heaven give you many, many merry days!
Good husband, let us every one go home,
And laugh this sport o'er by a country fire;
Sir John and all.

FORD   Let it be so. Sir John,
To Master Brook you yet shall hold your word;
For he tonight shall lie with Mistress Ford.   *Exeunt.*

---

229 *eschewed* refused, avoided   231 *muse* grumble, worry